All Earth Is Waiting

Good News for God's Creation at Advent

Katie Z. Dawson

ALL EARTH IS WAITING

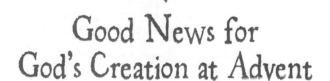

Good News for God's Creation at Advent

Abingdon Press / Nashville

ALL EARTH IS WAITING
GOOD NEWS FOR GOD'S CREATION AT ADVENT

This book is printed on elemental chlorine-free paper.
Library of Congress Cataloging-in-Publication data has been requested.
ISBN 978-1-5018-3982-5

17 18 19 20 21 22 23 24 25 26—10 9 8 7 6 5 4 3 2 1
MANUFACTURED IN THE UNITED STATES OF AMERICA

CONTENTS

INTRODUCTION

As the Advent season begins, the weather in my part of the world turns to winter. Last year the cold was slow to come, and so I found myself enjoying a balmy sixty-degree day at the end of November.

Typically, I try to put away my garden long before that point, but it had been a really busy fall. So I spent much of the unusually warm day working, weeding, clearing out what remained. And then, I planted.

Perennials like tulips, daffodils, and crocuses are not planted in the spring, but before the cold season. They are set deep in the earth when everything is brown and dead. So on that November day, I opened up the bags I had carefully stored containing those bulbs. I dug over two hundred little holes in my landscaping and buried those white bulbs with the red papery covering in the cold dirt.

And then I worked to divide other plants in my landscaping: the sedum, irises, and black-eyed susans. I chopped each plant in two with my shovel, and then I created a new home for each half.

I also trimmed down the stalks from the bee balm and milkweed plants and let the seeds that remained scatter in an area where I hoped they might grow next year. With this work of tending, the plants I set out a few years before will continue to multiply across our garden.

By the end of the day, my shoulders ached. My cheeks were red from the sun that had shone down all day long. And my hands were covered in blisters, even though I faithfully wore my gloves.

When I woke up the next day, there was very little evidence of the work I had done, aside from that which I carried in my body.

I had to wait.

There was nothing more I could do.

I trusted that on the other side of winter, tender green shoots would push themselves up through the last snow. I believed that the dark brown earth would yield to the vibrant magentas and yellows now hidden out of sight.

I stopped. I breathed. With my heart singing, I hoped.

In Hebrew, the words *wait* and *hope* share a common root. At the core of each, no matter the language, is the idea of expectation, and Advent is the season of expectation. In the Christian tradition, this season invites us to prepare our hearts—and not just for the birth of the child in Bethlehem. We are invited to wait and hope for that future day of salvation when Christ will come once again, bringing the kingdom of God that has no end.

Behind this longing, this expectation, this hope, is recognition that things are not the way they should be and a vision that draws us forward into the future. Filled with this vision, we cannot be content to sit back passively for it to happen. We are invited to live as people of the already, but not yet. We are invited to share the good news of God's kingdom with others and to live lives worthy of its calling, even as we wait.

Too often, we limit that glorious vision to human experiences and individual souls. But as we will explore together, God's story of restoration encompasses the whole of creation. All the earth waits with us for the coming of Christ and the kingdom of God. The good news we claim is also good news for every rock, hill, and plain; every sheep, cow, and dove; every breeze, raindrop, and star in the sky.

All around us, heaven and earth are pointing to the coming of Christ. Are we paying attention? Can we see the suffering and brokenness of this planet and how it longs for redemption? Are we listening to what heaven and earth tell us about the restoration and new creation that Jesus will usher in? This Advent, I invite you to open your heart to hear the good news of God for all the earth. Together, let us hear the call to respond and care not only for one another, but for the whole creation, as we await Christ's return.

In the five weeks of this study, we will first explore the longing and suffering of creation and why it hopes for God's children to embrace care of this world as our task. Then we will ask whether we are abusing the resources of this creation and how we might clear the way for God's will to be done. In the third week, we will explore the abundance and joy of the land and how to embrace God's gifts, especially in the food that we prepare and eat. In the fourth week of Advent, we will turn our attention to other living beings and ask how God's vision of peace might be realized in our relationships with animals. And finally, as we celebrate the birth of Christ, we will ask what it might mean for heaven and earth to be united through the presence and power of God.

I have come to see the act of setting out the flower bulbs each year as an Advent spiritual practice. It is a reminder of the cycle of life and death, but brings with it a glimpse of resurrection. It is an act of faith. With a vision of beauty and life, I am actively bringing color and habitat into the world. But, as I dig my fingers deep in that cold soil, I am reminded also of the fragility and longing of creation. When the warm weather arrives every year, I discover that some of the bulbs I took the time to plant in the fall will have rotted in the ground. Some will have been eaten by deer and squirrels. Every spring I discover that not all the bulbs have bloomed. This world is not as it should be, and all the earth longs for restoration and wholeness.

This Advent, let us stop and listen to heaven and nature sing. Let us explore what we have in common with this earth. And let us discover together what it might mean to share the good news with this planet. Our salvation is intimately connected with the redemption of this world, so may we find ways to live lives worthy of God's kingdom.

Not all the bulbs have bloomed.

All earth is waiting.

Chapter One

THE SOURCE OF HOPE

*The whole creation waits breathless with
anticipation for the revelation of God's sons and
daughters. Creation was subjected to frustration,
not by its own choice—it was the choice of the
one who subjected it—but in the hope that the
creation itself will be set free from slavery to
decay and brought into the glorious freedom of
God's children. We know that the whole creation
is groaning together and suffering labor paints
up until now.*

(Romans 8:19-22)

Long before our traditions around Christmas took hold, there
were other festivals in the Northern Hemisphere. The summer
had brought growth. The fall was a time of harvest, celebration,
and storage. And then the work was done, and people prepared
to tuck in for the next season. Winter brought barren earth, and
the nights were long, dark, and cold.

As Gayle Boss reflected upon these early traditions, she noticed a theme of fear—and a response to that fear—emerge: "they watched the light dwindle, felt the warmth weaken...as the sun sank and sank to its lowest point on their horizon, they felt the shadow of primal fear—fear for survival—crouching over them."[1] They began to search for an answer to the fears growing in their hearts. In the midst of that impending darkness, people needed a source of hope.

And so around the time of the winter solstice, the darkest night of the year, people lit ritual fires to remember that spring would come again. The Christian faith connected these practices with the birth of Jesus Christ, the light of the world. We began celebrating the birth of Christ during this time of the year and celebrated its approach as Advent, a season not of dread but of hopeful expectation. We embraced the yule log and the evergreen as signs of resurrection, eternal life, warmth, and light. As the hymn goes, "in the bleak midwinter" the source of our hope was born.

The Archbishop of Denver, Charles J. Chaput, defines hope as a choice, "a selfimposed discipline to trust in God while judging ourselves and the world with unblinkered, unsentimental clarity."[2] Hope is not a naïve sentiment or wishful thinking. The source of our hope is found at the intersection of our faithful trust in God and an unfiltered view of the reality that surrounds us. It doesn't shrink away from problems or difficulties, but enters into them confident that God will be there and will bring order, life, and joy out of the chaos.

When we truly look around with "unblinkered, unsentimental clarity," we discover that the planet around us is caught up in the same cycles of life and death, creation and destruction that we human beings are. These cycles are marked by the annual turning of the seasons that inspired fear and longing at the darkest, coldest times of the year. They are also evident in increasingly severe weather patterns: winter storms, flash flooding, droughts, and wildfires that wreak havoc and result in the destruction of nature, homes, businesses, and life. We recognize that the world around us often opposes life and harmony, and we trust that God will bring about something more.

Scientifically, the various seasons and weather we experience have to do with our position on the planet, the tilt of the axis of the earth, and our revolution around the sun. In my part of the world, plants sprout, grow, wither, and die, only to repeat the cycle endlessly year after year. I find that rhythm to be holy and good. Every winter is a time of Sabbath stillness that can be peaceful and beautiful, and then the turning of the season brings life out of the midst of death. Every spring is a glimpse of resurrection. Yet I am reminded of Gayle Boss's words that there is a sense of fear we also connect with the cold and barren times of the year. There is sadness in this time of ending, loss, and death. And so this is in particular a season when we reflect upon the longing in our hearts—and the promise within our faith—for an end to that cycle and the arrival of the abundant, everlasting life of God's kingdom.

When we imagine in our hearts what the kingdom of God might entail, too often we limit our vision to humanity only. Yet, as the Apostle Paul writes, "the whole creation waits breathless with anticipation ... [to] be set free from slavery to decay ... the whole creation is groaning together and suffering labor pains up until now" (Romans 8:19-22).

The vision of the God's kingdom that we hold in our hearts is a fulfillment of God's plan for the whole creation. Theologically, we are invited to imagine that the kingdom of God we prepare for every Advent season is a restoration of God's intention for the entire earth. It is the new creation. The story of faith we tell is about how the goodness and harmony of the original creation was broken and how Christ will knit it all back together. Advent calls all people of faith to not only wait for that Kingdom, but to actively bring it into being.

As I look out my window on a typical late-autumn day, most of the trees are bare aside from the pin oaks and evergreens. The sun is shining, but snow is predicted for the weekend. The wind chill is slightly below zero and when I stop and listen, I can hear the breeze blowing over the top of the chimney.

What might it mean for the whole creation to be waiting for the promise of abundant life?

The Stories of Creation

This world (and all that is in it) is so central to our faith that we have not one, but multiple stories of how this world was created in our sacred texts. In this study, we will explore from many angles the words of Genesis chapters 1 and 2 as we seek to understand God's intention for all of creation. It is amazing how these two chapters hold in tension two very different accounts, as well as the ways they deviate from the theories of modern scientific knowledge. Yet these Creation stories are each a powerful statement of faith based on what the writers knew about the natural world in which they lived.

At least for the two stories we find in Genesis, the authors didn't simply rely upon faith traditions, but looked around and observed everything they saw before they began to speak about the Creation. That is our task as well. We are called to seek the God we find in these texts and the claims they make about the created world and our place in it. And we are called to hold that wisdom alongside the knowledge of this world that grows and expands every day.

The first Creation story in Genesis (1:1–2:4a) tells us there was order and intent and purpose behind all that was made. Compared with other ancient myths where the cosmos is created out of violence and chaos, accidents and destruction, the God we claim acts with care and precision. Everything that results is good and holy.

In the second Creation story of Genesis (2:4b-25), we are invited to think more about the relationships involved: between God and humanity, humanity and nature, and human beings with one another. It highlights the interconnection of every living thing. We come from the topsoil. The plants and trees feed us. We are commanded to farm the garden and care for it. The animals are created for companionship and help for the first human until finally God forms the perfect companion from the very bones of the human's body. Every living thing is created by God to be intimately connected with every other. We simply cannot exist apart from the creation.

Together, these Creation stories in our Scripture invite us to believe that every single part of this creation is in the hands of the Creator and that every piece of this planet tells of God's goodness. As Jesus replies to the protestation of the Pharisees when the disciples sing praises, "If they were silent, the stones would shout" (Luke 19:40). Or, as we sing in the popular Christmas carol "Joy to the World," "heaven and nature sing....fields and floods, rocks, hills, and plains repeat the sounding joy."

Yes, the rocks would shout with joy if we were quiet. And if we stopped to listen, to pay attention, we just might hear the dirt speak. We just might hear each piece of creation telling of God's goodness.

Or we might hear the planet groaning. We might hear it tell us that those ideals of our Creation stories have been distorted by sin.

All earth is waiting.

The Cause of Frustration

Before I heard a call to ministry, I wanted to be a meteorologist.

As a child, I got sick to my stomach whenever there was a bad storm. My heart began to race and I got queasy. My whole body was filled with anxiety. While my childhood fear of storms seemed irrational, it actually led me to develop an interest in the weather. The more I learned about how clouds were formed and the impact of high or low pressure systems, the better I felt. That knowledge turned my apprehension into appreciation. And so I have learned to take seriously the science behind our climate and the impact of subtle changes in temperature, pressure, and wind streams.

We tend to limit our reflection upon questions of climate change or creation care to the scientific realm. And I know that there are some in this world who are skeptics about the nature or causality of climate change based on an interpretation of those scientific findings. But science is not the only field where understanding creation is important. As we saw above, the Scriptures placed an emphasis on this as well. Today, I am not a meteorologist or a climate scientist, but a pastor. So I want to invite us to dive into the depth of our Scriptures and our theological tradition. They also have something profound to say about the created world in which we live.

One of our guides this week is the Apostle Paul. Paul knew first-hand what it meant to have his life turned upside down by the good news of Jesus Christ. He made it his life mission to preach the gospel of the kingdom of God. What we discover when we read Paul, and in particular his letter to the people of Rome, is that he believed our salvation and redemption are intimately connected with the world we live in.

First, Paul believes that creation itself tells us who God is but that we refuse to honor the God we meet in this world (Romans 1:18-25). The amazing gifts of creation, with all of its diversity and abundance, should have cultivated in us gratitude and a spirit of reverence and worship. But we have turned instead to idols. We were supposed to live out the image of God and care for this world, but instead we have used and abused one another and this planet. We have neglected the fundamental truth of creation: that we belong to God; that it all belongs to God.

And so Paul describes how, through the sin of Adam, death has come into the world (Romans 5:10-17). In the *New Interpreter's Bible* (Vol. X), N. T. Wright wrestles with the complexity of what this means as he comments upon this passage. He asks whether death truly was a stranger in the world before Adam's sin. And he wonders whether this passage is about human death only, or all the ways in which sin and death wreak suffering and corruption in our created world. As we will explore in this chapter, Scripture seems to indicate that our human actions have consequences for all of creation.

The theologian Joseph Sittler claims that "we are all within the grip of three mighty structures which are transpersonal, everlasting, and universal."[3] He names these as evil, demonic forces, and death itself. These are what have captured us, bound us by fear, and have us trapped in these natural laws of periodicity and violence. The very turning of the seasons, the decay of every person and living thing, the force that moves us toward "no" instead of "yes"—these are not God's intention for creation, but the reality of a post-Fall world.

Whatever was intended for the creation, with the tree of life and fertile land and those first humans holding dominion over it all, is not what we experience today. That first sin, that first rejection of God's intention for creation, has a lasting impact on the entire world. When we sin, we don't just imitate or repeat that original disobedience, but we behave according to a human disposition that has been fundamentally shaped by the first human sin. And it isn't just human nature that's been shaped by sin; the disposition of the whole created world has been altered and shaped by it as well.

Our faith explains the brokenness of creation by saying that when Adam and Eve ate of the forbidden fruit in the garden (Genesis 3:6-7), everything changed. We typically focus on the human impact of the Fall, but those consequences are for the entire planet. As the Lord God confronts Adam and Eve, there is not only punishment for the snake and the two humans, but for the very soil.

> *Cursed is the fertile land because of you;*
>   *in pain you will eat from it*
>   *every day of your life.*
> *Weeds and thistles will grow for you,*
>   *even as you eat the field's plants;*
> *by the sweat of your face you will eat bread—*
>   *until you return to the fertile land.*
>   *(Genesis 3:17-19a)*

"Fields and floods, rocks, hills, and plains repeat the sounding joy," Isaac Watts wrote. But he also captured in the lyrics of "Joy to the World" the longing of all creation for the curse of Genesis 3 to end. We hear the earth cry out every time we sing the words, "no more let sins and sorrows grow, nor thorns infest the ground."

Theologically, we are called to consider the idea that, because human life is interwoven with this planet, our sin impacts the welfare of creation. As the prophets reminded the people of God, natural disasters, droughts, and destruction often came in the wake of human transgression. We find these stories all throughout our Scriptures, such as this one from Isaiah:

> *The earth dries up and wilts;*
>   *the world withers and wilts;*
>   *the heavens wither away with the earth.*
> *The earth lies polluted under its inhabitants,*
>   *for they have disobeyed instruction,*
>   *swept aside law,*
>   *and broken the ancient covenant.*
>   *(Isaiah 24:4-5)*

It is easy to point to man-made disasters like oil spills, water contamination, and forest fires and see this connection. But perhaps too quickly we explain away those ancient texts that remind us that the earth, the world, the heavens suffer as a result of human sin. Our Scriptures invite us to consider that destructive acts of nature like deadly hurricanes are not necessarily God's will, but reminders of the brokenness of all of creation. Our faith invites us to be open to the possibility that it is the sins of humanity that cause the torrential rain to fall and the harsh winds to blow. Our selfishness has brought death into the world (Romans 8:6).

Creation is longing for redemption, Paul finally says in our focus verses for this week. And it "was subjected to frustration, not by its own choice—it was the choice of the one who subjected it—but in the hope that the creation itself will be set free from slavery to decay..." (Romans 8:20-21). As we connect the dots of this faith story, we discover that our grasping and disobedience subjected all of creation to forces beyond our control. Because of our sin, the whole of creation was subjected to frustration, enslaved by decay, and trapped in the cycle of life and death.

And all the earth is waiting to be set free.

Labor Pains and Good News

One of those consequences of human sin, according to Genesis 3:16, is labor pains: "I will make your pregnancy very painful; in pain you will bear children." Women all across the planet cry out in frustration, "Thanks, Eve." I had the same reaction for a long time.

And then I stumbled upon an image that took my breath away. It was drawn by Sister Grace Remington who is a member of the Cistercian Sisters of the Mississippi Abbey in my home state of Iowa.* The image, "Virgin Mary Consoles Eve," depicts Eve, clad only in the flowing locks of her hair and clutching a piece of fruit. Her leg is entwined in the grip of a snake, her head hung in shame. Evil, sin, and death are her legacy. It is our legacy. But with one arm, she reaches out and places her hand on Mary's belly.

Mary stands there full of grace and mercy. She gently touches the face of Eve as if to tell her it is OK. She holds her other hand over Eve's and together they feel and experience the life of the One who was coming to redeem and restore all of the creation.

Yes, there would be labor pains. Yes, there would be suffering: that child born at Christmas would give up his life for the sake of the world, and sorrow would pierce Mary's heart. But there was also hope. The groaning of birth was not the same as the curse proclaimed on both the land and the serpent. Rather, through the suffering, God's love for the world would become known.

When Paul writes about the groaning of creation and all of God's children, he describes that pain as nothing compared with the "coming glory that is going to be revealed to us" (Romans 8:18). And then in verse 22, he uses the Greek word *synōdinō* to portray this reality; a word used only once in Scripture to describe the agony of childbirth. Creation is suffering labor pains. Something new is about to be born.

---

* Prints of the image are available on the Abbey's website: http://www.monasterycandy
.com/Product_List?c=33.

In this season of Advent, that image of Eve and Mary fills my heart with possibility and invites me to hear the words of Romans 8 in a different light. So often, I hear the frustration and groaning of the text, instead of diving in to see the good news. Yes, the world around us is groaning, but they are labor pains. Creation itself is about to be delivered, to be released, to be set free to become what God fully intends for it. And as I think about what it might mean for us to embrace the hope of this season and share the good news with all of creation, the image of the midwife comes to mind.

The word itself simply expresses accompaniment, to be with (mid) the wife, or woman giving birth. But it has been used as well to describe one who helps to bring something into being or existence. That metaphor was used by the actor, Andrew Garfield, as he described his work; but Brenden Busse notes that it is the task of all people of faith. "The actor, as with all priestly people, stands before the truth and participates in its telling by way of their words and gestures, by enacting our sacred stories of redemption and love. In contemplating the birth of Christ, [they] came to know that . . . it is by our personification of love, by our humble service, that we become the love for which we long."[4] We are called to midwife, to bring into being by our actions, the kingdom of God we long for.

As people of faith, we are evangelists. We share the good news of God with this world, in the hope that more and more people will shed the selfishness of sin and turn their hearts to embrace God. In that sense, we believe that no person is a finished job, a static person, with his or her eternal fate written in stone. Evangelism requires the confidence that God isn't finished with someone yet. God isn't finished with the planet, yet, either. And so, the work of evangelism is the work of hope for all of creation.

But that doesn't mean it will be easy. Busse reminds us that "this midwifing of love into the world does not excuse us from the pain of labor.... It is the labor of love that saves us."[5] This is the spirit captured in the verses that follow our focus Scripture: "The Spirit of God is arousing us within. We're also feeling the birth pangs. These sterile and barren bodies of ours are yearning for full deliverance. That is why the waiting does not diminish us, any more than waiting diminishes a pregnant mother. We are enlarged in the waiting" (Romans 8:22-25, MSG).

We experience this as we walk alongside someone who is coming to faith in God, or when we journey with someone through addiction into recovery. You have to have an "unblinkered, unsentimental clarity" about the realities of sin and yet nevertheless trust that God can and will bring about redemption. We trust that ultimately the forces of sin, evil, and death have no power over our lives. And we trust that a child has been born in Bethlehem so that "creation itself will be set free from slavery to decay" (Romans 8:21).

Paul keeps pointing backward to Adam in his Letter to the Romans, because Adam shows us God's original design for humankind. In N. T. Wright's words, it lends "a particular shape to eschatological hope...in Christ the human project, begun in Adam but never completed, has been brought to its intended goal."[6] In the beginning, there was a part for all of humanity to play. We were not just supposed to tend the garden; we carry the image of God! And we have a role in what Terence Fretheim calls "intra-creational development, bringing the world along toward its fullest possible creational potential."[7]

We were supposed to help all of creation become its best possible self; and so now, as Christ is born into our lives and we claim the Spirit of God that sets us free, it is our task to take up that role again.

Paul tells the community of faith that we have an obligation to live as God's sons and daughters right here and right now. Not for our sake. Not for selfish reasons. But because all earth is waiting for us to do so. "The whole creation waits breathless with anticipation for the revelation of God's sons and daughters" (Romans 8:19). If we believe that we are called to share the love of God with those people who are subjected to sin and death and to love them as Christ first loved us, then why do we not also extend that love and care toward the earth? Or as Sittler asks, "Could [the whole creation] be waiting for the children of God to begin to act like they are?"[8]

Perhaps the historical person who exemplified this best is Saint Francis. Jack Wintz believes Saint Francis saw the birth of Jesus Christ into the world as the source of his love for all of creation because God was "entering not only the family of humanity but the whole family of creation, becoming one in a sense with the very dust out of which all things were made."[9] And Saint Francis told that story of redemption with the very way he walked upon this earth and his actions.

One day, he was traveling and saw a tree full of birds above him. So moved was he to share the good news of God's saving love that he began to preach: "Oh birds, my brothers and sisters, you have a great obligation to praise your Creator, who clothed you in feathers and gave you wings to fly with, provided you with pure air and cares for you without any worry on your part."[10] He didn't hesitate to share the good news of God with any part of this world. In fact, as a tangible act of that love, Francis encouraged people to scatter seed along the roads for birds on Christmas Day so that all of God's creatures might celebrate the birth of Jesus Christ into this world.

The life, death, and resurrection of Jesus Christ is the source of our hope. But the source of hope for this world is us. The whole creation is waiting for us to let go of our selfish ways and begin acting like the children of God. It is waiting for us to hold in our hearts a vision of an interconnected world and to remember that every part of this planet tells of God's goodness. It is waiting for us to see the sacred worth of the elements, the flora, the fauna, to live gently as stewards and protectors.

At the winter solstice, our ancestors turned to practices that cultivated hope in the midst of their fear. During Advent we turn to Christ, the hope we long for, and wait for his coming once again. In the midst of the groaning, fear, and suffering of creation today, we are called once again to practices that bring into being the hope of Jesus Christ, the hope of the new creation.

All the earth is waiting.

And it is waiting for you and for me.

Questions for Reflection and Discussion

1. How have you heard heaven and nature sing God's praises?

2. Hope requires "unblinkered, unsentimental clarity." Describe with this unfiltered view a way that you have heard creation groaning in your community.

3. Name an example of selfish behavior in your life that impacts the world around you. How could you be more selfless?

4. Sittler argues that all of creation is "in the grip of three mighty structures," including death itself. In the turning of the four seasons, we glimpse the hope and promise of God as life bursts forth from death every spring. In the vision of the new creation in Revelation, death will be no more, there will no longer be any curse (Revelation 21:4, 22:3). What would be different in your neighborhood if death was defeated for good?

5. What is a way that you might help bring about the fullest possible potential of some part of creation that is around you?

Prayer

Holy God, we trust that you formed this world out of goodness and love. We see your glory etched in every living thing. And yet, how often have we turned away from your gifts and sought our own selfish ways. How often have we chosen death over life! Help us, O God, in this season of Advent, to turn back to you. Fill us with your Spirit of hope so that in the face of the powers of this world we might once again choose to be guided by your purpose. Amen.

Focus for the Week

When we share the good news of God's kingdom with another person, the message sinks deeper if we take time to get to know who the person is and where he or she is struggling. Hope is born out of the reality of a person's brokenness. This week, take time to simply be present in the natural world. Take time each day to be outside and pay attention to what you experience. Look for the brokenness and for the glimpses of resurrection and redemption. Think about how you might work to bring about the fullest possible potential of nature in your neighborhood by planting trees in the spring, cleaning up an area, or by adding feeders for wild animals.

You might also remember St. Francis while you are out walking. Audubon holds a Christmas Bird Count each year (2017 will be the 118th annual Bird Count!) and you can gather together with people from your neighborhood or church to collect data about the birds in your community. Check it out at: www.audubon.org/conservation/science/christmas-bird-count.

Chapter Two

CLEAR THE WAY

A voice is crying out:
"Clear the LORD's way in the desert!
  Make a level highway in the wilderness for
  our God!
Every valley will be raised up,
  and every mountain and hill will be flattened.
  Uneven ground will become level,
  and rough terrain a valley plain."

(Isaiah 40:3-4)

Charlie Brown isn't so sure what Christmas is supposed to be about. As he watches all of the other children in the neighborhood in the TV special *A Charlie Brown Christmas*, he sees them focused on the wrong things and laments the over-commercialization of the holiday. Lucy wants real estate. His sister, Sally, wants money—lots of money. Even his dog, Snoopy, is caught up in it all.

To lift his spirits, Charlie Brown agrees to direct a Christmas play, but that starts to get out of control with excitement, fights, and props...including the request for a "big, shiny, aluminum tree." Reluctantly he searches for it and then discovers the only living tree in the whole lot. It is small and scraggly. The needles fall off when he picks it up. But Charlie Brown thinks it is perfect.

All the chaos and the clutter, the tinsel and the traditions can get in the way of remembering what the seasons of Advent and Christmas are truly all about. And so it is that the children leave the stage laughing over this ridiculously small tree. Charlie Brown throws his hands up in frustration: "Isn't there anyone who knows what Christmas is all about?"

Linus does. With only his voice and a spotlight on the nearly empty stage, he recites the annunciation to the shepherds from the Gospel of Luke. He clears away all the pretense and show and simply tells the story.

The season of Advent can be such a chaotic time of year, with holiday parties, shopping for gifts, and special events in churches and schools. This week, we have a chance to explore together what it might mean to clear a way in the midst of it all for the kingdom of God—to clear away the pretense and show and simply experience the story. Not just in our personal lives, but for all of creation.

Upending Expectations

One of the Scriptures that we often hear in our churches during this season is the Magnificat of Mary (Luke 1:46-55). As she ponders what it means for the Savior of the world to be carried in her womb, she casts a vision of the longing of hearts and minds:

> *He has pulled the powerful down from their thrones*
> *and lifted up the lowly.*
> *He has filled the hungry with good things*
> *and sent the rich away empty-handed."*
>
> *(Luke 1:52-53)*

The coming of our Savior promises to turn this world upside down.

Those words often have a difficult time finding a way into our hearts. While I don't often think about myself as the rich or powerful, I also know that I have far more wealth, technology, and comfort in my home office than others in this world will possess in their lifetime. And from a position of privilege, it is not always easy to be aware of how my resources have come at the expense of the planet and people. In fact, it often blinds me to my need for salvation and redemption. In his commentary, R. Alan Culpepper notes that the poor and hungry desperately need a savior, but "those who have power and means, privilege and position have no need sufficient to lead them to voice such a term that is itself a plea for help."[1] Power, means, privilege, and position must be cleared away before we can see the need for a savior or hear Mary's words as an expression of our longing.

But even as the mother of Jesus sings these words of praise, the child in her relative Elizabeth's womb is leaping for joy. That child would grow to become the man we know as John the Baptist. And in his ministry, he helps all of us, no matter our position, understand what it means to clear the way.

In those days John the Baptist appeared in the desert of Judea announcing, "Change your hearts and lives! Here comes the kingdom of heaven!" He was the one of whom Isaiah the prophet spoke when he said:

"The voice of one shouting in the wilderness,
'Prepare the way for the Lord; make his
paths straight.' "

(Matthew 3:1-4)

As John the Baptist enters the scene, the Gospel writer deliberately connects his ministry with the promises of Isaiah 40 and the role of preparation and clearing the way. He appears in all four Gospels as a prophet who shares the good news of God's kingdom. But he does so in a way that invites us to truly clear away all obstacles that come between us and faithfulness...including sin. He is not gentle with his words, but speaks the truth to people who have built up walls between themselves and God. Christopher Sietz claims that John's harsh preaching echoes Isaiah, in which "judgment and defeat are signs of God's clearing away the brush and dry rot that have kept God safely at a distance."[2] The Hebrew word used in Isaiah 40:3, *panah*, conjures the image of clearing the ground and preparing the soil by getting rid of all the rocks and roots before you plant. In the same way, John invites us to get our hearts and lives ready, to clear away all that has kept us from God, and to prepare the way for Jesus to enter our lives.

One of the ways he preaches this message is through his very lifestyle. As noted in the Gospels of Matthew and Mark, John the

Baptist wears strange clothes and eats unique foods (Matthew 3:4; Mark 1:6). His very life is reminiscent of the prophets of old, like Elijah (2 Kings 1:8). He intentionally separates himself from society and identifies "with the wilderness that was to be the scene of eschatological renewal."[3]

In other words, John let go of the expectations of his day in order to live in solidarity with the less fortunate and with creation itself, which he believed was God's intention for our lives. He chose to go out into the wilderness to discover God's glory. His ascetic nature stood in stark contrast to the powerful of Jerusalem and echoed the humble birth of Jesus Christ into the world. As he proclaimed that One was coming who would bring about God's kingdom, he called the people of the world to change their hearts and lives in order to clear the way for Jesus.

Buying Our Way to Christmas

We usually read about John the Baptist during the second week of Advent. This means that John's message of repentance and preparation often is heard in our churches during the same time of year we are setting out to fill Christmas wish lists. It is hard to reconcile either his words or his lifestyle with our consumer attitudes and behaviors surrounding Black Friday and Cyber Monday. According to the National Retail Federation (nrf.com /holiday), overall holiday sales for 2016 were around $658 billion, and individual consumers planned to spend over $900 on gifts, cards, food, decorations, and other things during the holiday season. Charlie Brown is right . . . somehow, we have made Advent, this season of expectation and preparation for the coming of Jesus Christ in our lives, into the season of consumerism.

I am the proud aunt to eight nieces and nephews, and one of the things I love to do is to give them something memorable each year. A few Christmases ago, I was able to purchase an American Girl doll, Samantha, from a friend who was parting ways with childhood possessions. I carefully wrapped that doll and included a note about how I had a Samantha doll when I was my niece's age, too. When she opened that box, she literally burst into tears of happiness. The joy as a child unwraps a package to discover something that "I've always wanted" is remarkable.

Last year, when we gathered with family in the living room, I watched as that spirit of generosity overtook the entire room. So many presents were piled around the children that they could no longer be seen. There were mountains of packages and shiny holiday bags precariously piled on the floor and on the arms of chairs and couches. And then we leveled them as the unwrapping began. We carted roughly five garbage bags of wrapping paper and toy packaging out of the house. The items that were given with such generosity barely fit into the vehicles of those families driving home.

I sat there in the aftermath, picking up bits of tape and paper that had been left behind, and wondered how many trees worth of paper and cardboard we had carried to the curb. And I wonder today how many of those toys and items are still being used and cherished.

It is so easy to get caught up in expectations like these that have absolutely nothing to do with the birth of Christ and the longing of the whole earth for salvation. In many cases, the consumer clutter of our lives is doing further damage to the creation around us and becomes a distraction or roadblock, rather than helping clear the way for the kingdom of God.

John the Baptist enters the scene in this second week of Advent with a call to change our hearts and our lives. Instead of spending our time and energy on the mindless consumerism of the season, this is the time to reflect upon the fruit that is being produced in our lives. The harsh words of John the Baptist remind us that when Christ comes, those who are not actively working toward the kingdom of God will be judged. Jesus himself will clear the threshing area and separate the wheat from the husks (Matthew 3:12).

Flattening Mountains and Filling Valleys

Life as we have grown accustomed to it in the United States depends upon resources hidden within the earth, like fossil fuels. From them, we get electricity and roads, synthetic rubber and fertilizer, and all things plastic. They are the backbone of all of that consumerism Charlie Brown was so concerned about at Christmastime. Yet, our excessive pursuit of these resources creates barriers toward God's redemption of the earth.

While our climate has varied over the ages, the intricate balance of life on this earth is supported by the earth's atmosphere and the balance of gases within it—such as nitrogen, oxygen, and carbon dioxide. This, in turn, depends partly on the natural storage of carbon in plant life through sequestration. Over time those plants decay and become fossil fuels, which also store the carbon. When we use those fuels, stored carbon is released into the atmosphere in the form of carbon dioxide. According to the Environmental Protection Agency, carbon dioxide is the main greenhouse gas influencing recent climate change. And human activities like burning fossil fuels and certain kinds of land use release high amounts of carbon dioxide into the atmosphere, causing the level of carbon dioxide to rise. Our choices are upsetting the balance.

It's not limited to the atmosphere. In fact, in a gross parody of the prophet's vision in Isaiah 40, we literally level the earth in order to extract natural resources. One example is mountaintop removal mining. In the 1960s, this new method of coal mining came into use and had the potential to be less dangerous than underground mining. It allows coal companies to blast the tops off of mountains with explosives, exposing the seams of coal from above. The debris is sorted and the waste dirt and rock, also known as overburden, is disposed of in nearby valleys or used to create a new ridge.

This method can be beneficial because it is an inexpensive and efficient way to meet the energy needs of life today. According to the U.S. Energy Information Administration, a third of all electricity generated in 2015 came from coal. And even as coal production has reduced some in the United States, overall energy consumption is expected to continue increasing by a projected 5 percent in the next two decades.

But there are harmful impacts of this method. Explosions used to break up the earth threaten birds and animals in the area. And the changes to the topography impact the environment as well. The U.S. Fish and Wildlife Service notes that some species are nearing extinction due to changes in the valley streams that are their habitat. Overburden often fills up valleys, which leads to the destruction of springs and streams and lowers the water quality in areas downstream.

There are also serious health impacts for miners. While the incidence of black lung among coal workers dropped drastically in the past few decades due to regulations, the rates of black lung today have returned to alarming highs. Surface miners were often exempt from many mining regulations, and the increased use of mountaintop removal means that those places where "mountaintop mining operations are largely concentrated...are also the places where the worst cases of black lung are clustered," according to a researcher at North Carolina State University.[4] In 2016, NPR broke the news that there have been at least 962 cases of complicated black lung (a more advanced form of the disease) in this decade, which is already two times as many as reported over the previous four decades combined.[5]

There are similarities between the desolation brought by such mining practices and the image of the wilderness that forms the backdrop for Isaiah 40. For the prophet and his audience, the wilderness is an abandoned and desolate place that represents not only the physical space between the Israelites and their homeland, but also the "graphic location of God's wrath in judgment."[6] The wilderness is all of those places where our sin, our arrogance, our pride has laid waste to creation. We believe that our power allows us to use creation as we will, but Christopher Sietz points out that Isaiah often references nations who misuse nature and as a result eventually receive God's wrath. One example is the Assyrian king, Sennacherib, who mocked God by felling the cedars of Lebanon and drying up the streams of Egypt and who was swiftly defeated (Isaiah 37).

Based on the background of this text, when the voice cries out to "Clear the LORD's way in the desert!" (Isaiah 40:3), I'm confident the prophet wasn't picturing mountains being stripped for energy production. When we look out upon the filled-in valleys of Appalachia, or notice the decline in water quality, or the subtle rise in temperature, we should be asking what God's word of judgment is for our time.

We need to acknowledge our failures, but let us also not forget that we worship a God of compassion and mercy who seeks redemption and restoration. In spite of the sins of the people of Israel, the prophet Isaiah was moved to share God's vision of salvation. He offered words of comfort into the midst of their trial and tribulation. But this was not only a message for the people living in exile; it was for all the earth. The wilderness, creation itself, is where Isaiah saw the in-breaking of God's kingdom.

In *The New Interpreter's Bible* (Vol. VI), Christopher Sietz reminds us that the wilderness is the very place where we first glimpse the glory of salvation. There will be flowers and rejoicing, life-giving waters, and a highway for the redeemed to walk safely into God's presence (Isaiah 35). The coastlands and the ends of the earth will take courage in the presence of God (Isaiah 41: 5-6). God will turn dry land into places of oasis and the creatures will honor the one who makes a way (Isaiah 43:19-20). When the day of salvation comes, the mountains will be turned into roads and pastures so that all of creation might come to feast and drink (Isaiah 49:9-12).

Words of comfort are spoken to Jerusalem, God's people, because "her compulsory service has ended...her penalty has been paid" (Isaiah 40:2). God was going to clear a way where there had been no way. God was going to remove every obstacle that represented judgment and waste and was going to transform and restore it. And this included creation itself.

Every valley will be raised up,
and every mountain and hill will be flattened.
Uneven ground will become level,
and rough terrain a valley plain.
(Isaiah 40:4).

What had been desolate would be the site of redemption and glory. Obstacles would be cleared away so that God's glory could be revealed.

Clearing the Clutter

A friend sat me down one afternoon and made me watch a video called "The Story of Stuff."* One of the statistics that really seared into my mind is that out of all the things we use in our economy—things we harvest, mine, move, or process in some way—*ninety-nine percent* of it becomes trash in six months or less.

Ninety-nine percent.

This stunning figure is not only about the disposable products we use every day, or the heaps of debris after Christmas, but also includes the waste generated as we extract resources, in production, packaging, transportation, marketing, and retail.

In my hometown of Cedar Rapids, Iowa, there is a landfill on the riverfront that first went into operation in the 1960s. We affectionately call it "Mount Trashmore." For over forty years, it has grown and expanded and is now about 208 feet tall and takes up 65 acres of land. To put that into context, that's as high as a 19-story building and takes up as much space as 50 football fields. Our discarded stuff is literally creating mountains.

---

* You can watch it at http://storyofstuff.org/movies/story-of-stuff/

Isaiah points us to that great day of salvation when the valleys will be raised and the high places flattened (Isaiah 40). As we look around at the world we have created, that vision points to the restoration of the pits we have dug in the earth to extract resources. It calls into being the day when the things we have piled into our landfills finally decompose and return to the ground. But above all, it is a challenge to clear our lives of the clutter that creates those mountains and valleys in the first place. We can choose a new way that can fulfill Isaiah's vision here and now.

That video from 2007 has now turned into *The Story of Stuff Project*, which educates people about the stuff we have, where it comes from, and how to be more responsible with its use. They even have free, downloadable faith-based programs for teens.* As one of the lessons tells students, prophets like John the Baptist were threatening to leaders of their day because they challenged the status quo and our deeply engrained habits of faith. Being presented with the reality behind our consumer impulses can generate the same kind of resistance. It is hard to come to terms with just how much we consume and throw away, much less what the impacts are for God's creation as a whole.

John the Baptist invites us to change our hearts and minds. He invites us to clear away anything that distracts us from God (including our stuff) and to focus on simply preparing the way for God's kingdom. He invites us to get down to the basics and live a life that is more in tune with the salvation God intends for the world.

Not all of us, however, are prepared to go live in the desert and eat locusts. And I'm not sure we have to. But we can think about

---

* You can find the resources at storyofstuff.org/resources.

the impact of our stuff. And we should find ways to focus less on consumer desires and more on what God desires.

One program that helps people to do this every year is Advent Conspiracy (www.adventconspiracy.org). It encourages people to worship more fully, spend less on gifts, give more presence, and to love like Jesus. Each year, they invite faith communities to consider making a commitment to living out those four values and to donate a portion of what they might have otherwise spent on holiday gifts to help bring clean water to the world.

There are also movements to embrace minimalism that can help us have an impact in our daily lives. From tiny homes to capsule wardrobes, people are embracing a life with less stuff and are finding that there is more joy and less stress as a result.

Many have been inspired by Marie Kondo's 2011 book, *The Life-Changing Magic of Tidying Up: The Japanese Art of Decluttering and Organizing*. The KonMari method that the book describes invites people to radically transform their lives by discarding the clutter that they live with—the superfluous possessions. The basic tool for doing so is asking a simple question: does the item spark joy? In the book, she talks about how the average client who uses her method will discard between twenty and thirty forty-five liter bags of stuff. Yet when they have done so, they are surprised to find that their daily lives continue with no added inconvenience.

Asking if something sparks joy in one's life can seem a very self-centered sort of exercise. However, from a faith perspective, maybe we should be asking something else. Are we going to cherish and appreciate the gifts of this planet, or are we simply going to use the resources of this earth and then throw them away, with no consideration of the long-term impact to the planet or our salvation? Maybe before we fill our homes with the clutter of Christmas presents and consumer goods that we really don't need, we should be asking a different simple question: how does my possession of this item or use of this resource spark joy for all of creation?

Blessed Are the Debonair

One of the theologians I have grown to love is Reverend Joseph Sittler. He was born in 1904 and in his work he began connecting Christian belief and environmental concerns as early as the 1950s. He firmly believed that creation care should be one of the central concerns of our faith, and so he asks different questions than many other theologians.* In one lecture, a talk from 1984 entitled "His God Story," he reflected upon the familiar beatitude, "Happy are people who are humble, because they will inherit the earth" (Matthew 5:5). Sittler's mind was drawn to his grandmother's Bible. She was from France and had a French translation of Scripture. She often would write Bible verses in the margins of letters, including the Beatitudes. Sittler remembered how this particular verse was translated in her Bible: "*Heureux les débonnaires,*" or "Blessed are the debonair."

Immediately, you probably have an image in your mind of what it means to be debonair. I know, for me, I pictured a gentleman in a top hat and a fancy tuxedo, bowing in a room with a fancy chandelier. Pretty much the opposite of meek or humble. Yet Sittler claims the word *debonair* in the French Geneva Bible would have described someone who was so centered that

---

* Many recordings of Sittler's lectures are available at www.josephsittler.org.

they didn't need status or wealth to provide for their sense of self-worth. Because of this, a debonair person could resist the temptations of worldly things. *Debonair* describes a sense of purpose, according to Sittler in his lecture, "in which you sit lightly on the offerings and temptations of this world because you have a vision of something better."[7] We often translate the Greek word used here by Matthew, *praus*, as humble or meek, but maybe other valid definitions like benevolent, gentle, and humane should be in focus as well.

This is who will inherit the earth. Not own or control or manipulate, but *inherit*. In other words, Sittler says in his talk, Jesus can be understood in this way: "Blessed are they of a gentle spirit because they live in the world not as ones who strut around as if they own the place.... Rather, their fist feeling for the world is one of tender wonder, gratitude, amazement."[8]

Tender wonder, gratitude, and amazement are precisely the words to describe the spirits of those who gathered alongside the Jordan River or who heard the words of God in the midst of their exile. As Isaiah proclaimed that their penalty had been paid, the people of Jerusalem recalled the wonder and majesty of their Creator (Isaiah 40:12-31). When the people responded to the call of John the Baptist to change their hearts and lives, they confessed their sins, letting go of their hold on the world and their way of doing things and opening themselves to the one who was coming (Matthew 3:2, 5-6).

In the same way, we are called to embody a spirit of gratitude as we remember that every little bit of this world was made by God and belongs to God; we are merely granted temporary guardianship and use. Adam and Eve are placed in the garden in Genesis to care for the earth. Creation was supposed to be thought of not as an obstacle to their goals and their faithfulness, but as an opportunity to express their faithfulness to God by caring for it.

In the same lecture, "His God Story," Reverend Sittler tells about a time when he saw this debonair spirit in action while taking some students on a hike through the Cascades. They were all caught up in their music and conversation until they walked into the woods, and then they grew silent. He noticed that they would reach out and touch the trees and he thought, "They inherit the world *because* they don't own it. They don't think of it fundamentally as potential two-by-fours, though it's all right to use it that way wisely; if you love a thing, then you're prepared to use it wisely."[9]

So this season of Advent we are invited to cultivate a spirit that would help us understand creation not as a resource to be plundered, but as a gift. Instead of gouging new valleys, piling high mountains of waste, or leveling the earth for our own ends, we should open ourselves up to experience the presence of God as we make our way in harmony with the world. Henri Nouwen describes how prayer can help create that openness: "in place of manipulating, he who prays stands receptive before the world. He no longer grabs but caresses, he no longer bites, but kisses… nature can show itself completely renewed. Instead of an obstacle, it becomes a way."[10]

A prayer-filled life invites us to periodically check ourselves and ask if we have taken the gifts of this world for granted. It calls us to speak up when we see others abusing our common resources. It demands that we teach ourselves and our children how to walk gently and carefully along this precious planet.

One place we can start is by reconsidering how we let the stuff of the world and our impulse to buy get in the way of God's salvation. Let us clear the way for all the earth to experience the kingdom of God.

Questions for Reflection and Discussion

1. What is distracting you from hearing the message of Christmas this year?
2. What is a gift that you have always wanted? Did you receive it or not? What difference did that make in your life?
3. John the Baptist is not gentle, but he does speak the truth. In my family, we sometimes have "come to Jesus moments," or interventions, when some difficult reality needs to be brought to the surface. What is hard to hear about this message of consumerism?
4. How could you give fewer presents and more presence this year?
5. Matthew 5:5 invites us to think about what it means to inherit, rather than own the earth. How are you preserving and protecting creation so that future generations can inherit this gift?

Prayer

Holy God, you have promised to provide a way toward our salvation, clearing away everything that we have put between us. We are challenged by the reminder that you turn this world upside down, humbling the powerful and lifting up the lowly.

Help us, in this season of Advent, to open ourselves to your world, so that we might receive all of creation as a gift to be shared, rather than an object to be consumed. Amen.

Focus for the Week

Each of us leaves a "carbon footprint" on the world based on our use of various resources. One faithful response is to explore what your footprint is and then seek ways to reduce the impact you leave. This can apply to our churches as well. My congregation in Des Moines is a "Cool Congregation," part of an effort by religious communities to respond to global warming through thoughtful use of resources. One action we have taken is to convert all of our external building lights to LED, which not only helps protect our natural resources, but has also had a drastic impact on our energy bill!

As you decorate for the holiday season, consider how less might be more and what it might mean to make a smaller impact on the environment. Consider switching, like my church, to more energy-efficient strands of lights. And think about the impact of your Christmas tree. If you use a live tree, consider mulching it afterward to provide replenishment of resources for your landscaping. If you choose an artificial tree, know that if you use it for more than a decade, you might leave a smaller total carbon footprint.

Take some time this week to check out the resources at http://www.coolcongregations.org/calculator/ and find out the carbon footprint of both your church and individual households. The Environmental Protection Agency also has a calculator that can be found at https://www3.epa.gov/carbon-footprint-calculator/.

Chapter 3

Discovering Joy

Yet even now, says the Lord,
return to me with all your hearts,
with fasting, with weeping, and with sorrow;
tear your hearts
and not your clothing....
Don't fear, fertile land;
rejoice and be glad,
for the Lord is about to do great things!

(Joel 2:12-13, 21)

In my family, you can't have Christmas without the holiday baking. Every year, the women in my mom's family made candies and cookies, bars and balls, and filled the kitchen with laughter, stories, and a healthy dusting of flour. Even my grandpa got in the mix with his famous five-pound fudge.

When I was a child, my mom brought this tradition home to us. There would be a weekend or two about this time of year when every pan, pot, and cookie sheet would be commandeered for making treats. We slathered on the filling and then rolled up and sliced the date pinwheel cookies. We sat for hours unwrapping individual Rolos so that we could place them inside of shortbread dough and bake them. When they cooled, we dusted them with powdered sugar and promptly devoured them. We watched the buttery syrup on the stove rise to just the right temperature so that we could pour it over the club crackers carefully laid in the jelly roll pan, where it would soak in and harden and become my absolute favorite holiday treat.

Now that my siblings and I are all grown up, we still try to find an afternoon to gather and make a few of the favorites. At our extended family Christmas, everyone brings the few items that are their specialty, and we place them all on a table and divide up the goodies.

There is something about food that brings people together. At the holidays, as the tables are spread with baked goods and roasted meats, vegetables mashed or sautéed with fatty goodness, and heaps of desserts, community is born. We might argue over politics or give one another a hard time about what we are doing with our lives, but we take the time to be there with one another. It matters that we can sit at the same table and pass the rolls and look one another in the eye.

Maybe this is why one of the central images of our faith is the table of Jesus Christ. In Communion, as we break the bread of life and share the cup of salvation, we have a glimpse of the heavenly banquet. Even as Jesus blesses the meal, we find ourselves remembering the ancient promise of Isaiah:

The Lord of heavenly forces will prepare for
all peoples
   a rich feast, a feast of choice wines,
   of select foods rich in flavor....
This is the LORD, for whom we have waited;
   let's be glad and rejoice in his salvation!"
                       (Isaiah 25:6, 9)

Over and over again in the Gospels, God's kingdom is portrayed as a feast, as a big party, with people from far and wide invited to sit at the table (Matthew 8:11-12, 22:2-6, 25:1-10; Luke 14:16-20; John 7:37-38).

We are waiting for that banquet; we are waiting for that day of salvation. The great feast signals the arrival of that moment when "he will swallow up death forever.... / He will remove his people's disgrace from off the whole earth" (Isaiah 25:8). We are waiting for a new age where the power that death exercises over life will be no more.

All earth is waiting, too.

Fear Not!

We turn to the prophets of the Hebrew Scriptures so often in this season of Advent, because their words hold in front of us the vision of hope, restoration, and promise for salvation. But I am increasingly struck as I read the prophets how integrated their view of restoration and God's kingdom was. The Christian faith today so often slips into a focus on the individual soul, but the words of Scripture expand our vision not only to other people, but to all of creation.

In our focus Scripture for this week, Joel proclaims hope for the soil and what grows from it: "Don't fear, fertile land; rejoice and be glad…. / Don't be afraid, animals of the field, for the meadows of the wilderness will turn green" (Joel 2:21, 22). He shares a vision of the blessings of the earth spilling over to all of creation as the harvests increase, and all people experience the abundance of God. On the day of salvation, "the mountains will drip sweet wine, / the hills will flow with milk, / and all the streambeds of Judah will flow with water" (Joel 3:18).

The joy-filled word of the Lord came to Joel in the midst of a devastating plague of locusts (Joel 1:2-4). Elizabeth Achtemeier reminds us that "it was the function of the prophet to tell, on the basis of the Word of God, just where and when God was at work."[1] As Joel witnessed the disaster around him, he interpreted it through the lens of the word he had been given. While our modern sensibilities do not typically connect natural disasters with the wrath of God, throughout the Scriptures, our creating God uses nature as a means of punishment and to call the people to repentance.

When the laws were first given to Moses and the Israelites, future curses were promised for those who "don't obey the LORD your God's voice by carefully doing all his commandments and his regulations" (Deuteronomy 28:15)—including locusts that destroy harvests (Deuteronomy 28:38). In Joel's time, an army of insect invaders ruined vines and trees, leaving the ground in mourning (Joel 1:6-12). Joel lifts up no specific details about the sins of the people that brought on this devastation, but instead shares the call to return to the Lord (Joel 2:12).

While the Lord's judgment had been great, as the people returned to God, "the LORD became passionate about this land,

and had pity on his people" (Joel 2:18). God will restore the land and the people. In the midst of suffering, oppression, and judgment, it is often difficult to receive God's promises without trepidation. Yet, Joel encourages not only the people, but all of creation to set aside fear and to hear the good news.

As Achtemeier tells us, the "Fear not!" imperative Joel uses echoes Isaiah 41:10. We hear in those words the promise that the presence of God brings strength into the midst of our adversity.[2] I am reminded of the words of comfort spoken by the angels to Mary and the shepherds in the annunciations of Christ's birth (Luke 1:30; 2:10). They might not have been the ones the world celebrated, but in Advent, we remember God "shows mercy to everyone...has lifted up the lowly...has filled the hungry with good things....[and] has come to the aid of his servant Israel" (Luke 1:50-54). A plague of locusts might have destroyed the land and the surrounding nations might be whispering, "Where is their God?" (Joel 2:17), but what Joel proclaims is good news, and it is not only meant for the people, but for nature, too.

The Soil Rejoices

Joel's vision moves beyond the plagued land of the moment to when "the great and dreadful day of the LORD comes" (Joel 2:31). The very presence of God will "settle down in Zion" (Joel 3:17). This ground, this fertile land, is the place of salvation. It has not been forgotten by God and it should not be forgotten by us.

In our focus Scripture, the word for "fertile land" in Hebrew is *adamah,* and it is the same word used in Genesis 2:7, where "the LORD God formed the human [*adam*] from the topsoil of the fertile land [*adamah*]." The soil, the ground, the dirt from which we were created also has reason to rejoice. It, too, is a part of the abundant life that God will restore in the new creation.

I grew up on a farm and often helped my grandparents in their garden, so there is a huge part of my soul that is fed by playing in the dirt. In 2015, I had an opportunity to take a year-long continuing education course called "Organic Ministry." Each month we gathered to learn about how the good news of God was taking root in the world that surrounds us. In the process, I discovered just how much I didn't know about soil, food production, and sustainability.

One of our primary texts for the class was *The Third Plate: Field Notes on the Future of Food*, by Dan Barber. Barber is not an environmentalist or a theologian, but a chef. He has grown to believe that attentive, quality farming and good food are tightly bound together. What he has discovered along his journey is that the future of food lies in activity that builds a sustainable food production system from the ground up. When we care for every part of the process, from the soil to the water to the seed, we are in fact creating more delicious and healthier food. In Joel, God poured out abundant rain in order to bring back the fertility of the soil and it resulted in feasts of grain, wine, and oil (Joel 2:23-24). When the soil is blessed, the people are, too.

Yet, our current food production system seems to have forgotten that truth. Barber quotes Wendell Berry who said, "We came with visions, but not with sight. We did not see or understand where we were or what was there, but destroyed what was there for the sake of what we desired."[3] Mass production of food in many ways is built upon getting as much as possible out of the ground. We fight against nature, stripping the land of every good nutrient in the process. We harm, rather than bless, the soil. Success looks like a good harvest and abundant production; too often we pay little regard to what we have sacrificed in our manipulations. Instead of seeing the diverse and rich resources of this world as a gift, we have manipulated the earth to produce what we think we want. The way we eat today is destroying the world around us.

The soil beneath our feet, the adamah, is alive. We think about dirt as dead matter, but in reality it is organic—full of both living and dead organisms. Fungi and bacteria help break down matter into soil, and animals such as earthworms churn and nurture the earth. Without all of that living and breathing of the soil, life as we know it would cease. And the soil can sustain itself and create more and more abundant life; it becomes more fertile through natural processes. Barber reflects upon this process and notes that "what's not eaten either nourishes new grass or becomes humus, a kind of long-term bank account that provides for the future needs of plants."[4]

But in the process of farming the land, we take fertility out of the soil. Too often we cannot put enough back into the soil to replace what we have taken. As a farm girl, I thought I understood this truth, because I know that we can't simply plant corn in the same field every single year and expect the harvest to increase. A simple practice like including beans in the crop rotation ensures that vital nutrients like nitrogen are returned to the soil. Allowing animals to graze on the land also helps because they naturally leave behind manure which helps fertilize the soil. But both of those take time, and chemical alternatives that can be sprayed upon the fields are a far more efficient way of meeting market demands.

David Montgomery noted, "Faith in the power of chemicals to catalyze plant growth replaced agricultural husbandry and made both crop rotations and the idea of adapting agricultural methods to the land seem quaint...large-scale agro-chemistry became conventional farming."[5] Many farmers today focus on just three nutrients out of the vast complexity of the living soil—nitrogen, phosphorus, and potassium—replace them chemically, and forget about the rest. Then we take that soil and focus on a few strains of grain that produce abundantly. We process them in ways that focus on shelf-life and stability and we stock our pantries.

All of those holiday treats my family prizes wouldn't exist without corn syrup and packaged flour. Yet what I discovered in my Organic Ministry class is that by processing all of these grains, we often are stripping them of the very substance that makes them healthy. One simple example is what we have done to wheat.

That sack of pure white flour sitting on your shelf today used to be kernels of wheat that each contained three parts: the germ, or seed; the starchy endosperm; and the bran, or seed coat. When the germ is crushed, it releases oils that turn the flour rancid within days, so the roller mills of the late 1800s figured out a way to separate the germ and bran leaving just the endosperm. Our flour today is shelf-stable, but no longer contains the bran or the germ. It is missing about 80 percent of its nutritional benefits. Barber notes that "the roller mills might have finally achieved a truly white flour, but the dead, chalky powder no longer tasted of wheat—or really of anything at all. We didn't just kill wheat. We killed the flavor."[6]

This is the same kind of behavior that prompted God to bring judgment upon the people in the time of Joel. When Achtemeier reflects upon the prophet's words, she notes that the people "tried to make God unnecessary, turning to other sources for life" and that we brought upon ourselves in the process, "sterility, hopelessness, lack of joy, and a threat of annihilation."[7] Yet, the Lord speaks to Joel and shares a vision of another way. Joel calls upon the people to return to the Lord and begs the people to gather, fast, and weep (Joel 2:15-17a). Together, they turn away from their failures and turn back to God, trusting that the Lord is "merciful and compassionate, / very patient, full of faithful love, and ready to forgive" (Joel 2:13). God hears their cries and as a result, the soil can set aside its fears and rejoice.

There is another way for us, too. Joseph Sittler wrote that "use is blessed when enjoyment is honored… and a world sacramentally received in joy is a world sanely used."[8] We can gather together and examine the practices we share, asking whether they help honor God's vision of creation. We can choose to live and eat in such a way that not only brings joy to our hearts and homes, but also brings about the restoration of the very soil that gives us life. One way that we can embrace Joel's vision for the blessing of creation—for the blessing of the soil itself—is by letting go and paying attention.

Paying Attention

One of the staples on our holiday dinner table is sweet corn. There is nothing better than the juicy, golden kernels of fresh Iowa corn in the middle of summer; but a close second is the corn we freeze and put away for winter. Near the middle of August, my in-laws buy bushels of sweet corn and spend an entire weekend cutting the kernels off the cob, lightly cooking them in a pan with butter, and then bagging them up to store in the freezer. It brings to mind memories from my childhood when I would run down to my grandma's basement storage at the holidays and bring up the jars of peaches and pickled beets and beans that we had canned the summer before.

One of my goals has always been to have my own garden where I could provide food for my family all year long, eating fresh produce during the summer and freezing or canning it for the winter. We moved to a new city about three years ago, and the garden I have started here has not been producing nearly as much as I had hoped. The rabbits ate all the green beans. The peas never came up. It was not warm enough for the peppers and they never flowered to bear fruit. The raspberries we planted when we moved in have only given us a handful of berries. Only the tomatoes have ever produced enough fruit for us to can and freeze.

One of the biggest problems in my garden is that the soil itself isn't very healthy. It is not that fertile land, adamah, that will bring forth abundant life. But with time, it can be. As Barber reflected upon what it meant to farm in a sustainable way, he discovered the idea that we could "grow nature" by encouraging what we find where we are. Yet to do so involves a bit of faith and trust, because the more we give up to nature the less control we have. Rather than manipulating our world, we should observe our land, pay attention to what it is telling us, and adapt accordingly.

One of the narratives around the season of Advent and Christmas is the journey of the magi to Bethlehem. I have always marveled at the way these strangers from a foreign place were willing to leave their homes because of a star. But they were people who paid deep attention to what the world around them was saying, and they responded accordingly. They found meaning and purpose in those stars above them and let the stars guide their way. There was no way of knowing where they would end up or what exactly they would discover when they got there. Yet as we read in the Gospel of Matthew, "the star they had seen in the east went ahead of them until it stood over the place where the child was. When they saw the star, they were filled with joy" (Matthew 2:9-10).

When we pay attention to our gardens or farms or to nature itself, we, too, discover unexpected gifts. We can allow the earth to guide our actions, rather than trying to force something unnatural. One of the things I learned during my Organic Ministry class was to let the weeds, rather than the stars, take me on a journey.

I always thought there were three options when it came to weeds. First, you could spray chemicals on them and hope they die, but potentially make your garden unsuitable for growth that season. Second, you could use more natural methods like pouring vinegar or hot water over the plants to cause them to wither. Or third, you could use some manual labor, get down on your hands and knees like my grandpa, and take them out by hand.

But in that class, I learned a fourth option: learn from the weeds. A weed is simply a plant that is growing where we don't want it. And that weed is growing and thriving in that particular soil because the conditions promote its growth. So whatever weed you find in your dirt can tell you what the soil is lacking, or what types of plants you should be growing there instead.

Dandelions can indicate that the soil is acidic, so perhaps instead of trying to grow lettuce or beans, you might want to plant some blueberries or potatoes. Or, you could work to improve the soil conditions by adding dolomitic limestone or compost to make the soil more neutral.

Chicory is a sign that the ground is too hard and compacted. You can break up the soil by planting sweet clover that will help break up the soil and replenish nitrogen. Or plant things in the brassica family like broccoli and cabbages, and then the next year take care to work the soil only when it is dry.

We are so quick to fight with nature instead of paying attention to what it needs and what might allow the earth around us to flourish. If we shift gears and start to do a little bit more listening, then maybe our lives would not be so preoccupied with stamping out weeds or staring at dying plants. Instead we could focus on promoting growth, health, and vitality in the earth. We might might be able to both offer care and provide for the earth and discover amazing gifts along the way, much like Matthew's magi.

Practicing Dominion

In 2015, Pope Francis issued a letter to the world, *Laudato Sí*, translated as "Praise be to you." This letter calls upon all people to care for our common home, our sister, Mother Earth. I heard within his writing echoes of words put to paper by United Methodist bishops, in a pastoral letter from 2009 called *God's Renewed Creation: Call to Hope and Action.*

In both, we are reminded of the relationship between living organisms and their environment. We are reminded of our need to take the time to understand our ecology, the interconnected system of water, air, soil, plants, animals, and ourselves.

From the fight over water rights in California to the conflict being experienced in Iowa over nitrate levels in the water supply, the nation is full of stories about how the environmental choices we make in one location impact the whole of creation in another. And it is a complicated equation.

In my community in Iowa, there is a lawsuit being waged against counties farther north because runoff from fertilizer on farms has impacted the water supply in the city. But the reality is that this is not just about the practices of farmers upstream. Each of them is only responding to the demands of the market, which is impacted by our choices as consumers. It is easy to point fingers, but far more difficult to take responsibility for how our desire for hamburgers and preference for wheat over barley or oats has a negative impact on the ecology of our world.

In contrast, our faith calls us to respond to God's creation in a more receptive, attentive, and life-affirming way. We learn in the Creation stories of Genesis that we were made by a creative and life-giving God. Everything has a purpose. Everything is a gift and nothing was made by our own hands. Therefore, the foundation of our relationship with God should be one of gratitude. Gratitude for every breath we take, every drop of water we drink, every creature in the multitude of this diverse, beautiful planet.

Our relationship with the Creator is also fundamentally related to our relationship with the creation, because God calls us to take care of this earth. As we hear in Genesis 1:28, we are commanded to "be fertile and multiply; fill the earth and master it. Take charge of the fish of the sea, the birds in the sky, and everything crawling on the ground."

We are called to "master" the earth and "take charge" of the animals. Other translations include words like "subdue" and "dominion" (KJV), "control" and "rule" (CEV). This language has led us to believe we are called to control, use, and have power over the world. It is ours, to do with it whatever our hearts desire. But, maybe we should consider those verses again.

In *THE MESSAGE* translation this verse contains instead the words be responsible. We are given this responsibility because we were made in the image of God. So we are to hold dominion over the creation in the same way that God would: in love, in creation, in fostering diversity, in nurturing life. In *Laudato Sí*, Pope Francis reminds us that dominion has to be held alongside the call to "till and keep" or to farm and care for the garden of the world (Genesis 2:15). We can responsibly use the resources of this earth while at the same time caring for them and protecting them.

Great farmers and master gardeners know that they have to care about the soil as much as they do what is planted in it. One must protect the earth in order to work it. And you must listen and pay attention to what the environment demands, and respond accordingly if you ever want to influence what might grow there.

In Barber's book, he describes how the plains in North America used to be a prairie with incredible biodiversity. The grasses, shrubs, and flowering plants were sustained by extensive root systems. These root systems stored nutrients and energy, enabling the grasses to grow quickly and flourish. At the same time, the grass held the soil and prevented erosion as bison roamed and fertilized it. Over thousands of years, the soil developed a natural bank of fertility, which helped the plant life continue to thrive.

But we wanted to live on the prairie and grow food there. We broke up the deep roots of the perennial grasses with farm equipment and replaced them with the shallow root systems of annual wheat and other grains. The roots had held the soil together and helped prevent erosion, and they had also loosened up the soil so that oxygen could filter through the ground, helping provide fertile and sustainable land. The new, widespread farming changed the soil.

In the 1930s, nearly 75 percent of the United States experienced a decade of drought that devastated agriculture. In many ways, those farmers experienced the same kind of natural destruction that had been wrought by the locusts in Joel. Only, in their case, the vegetation that brought life to the soil withered from lack of moisture, instead of by the teeth of an army of locusts (Joel 1:6-7). Without the deep prairie roots to hold the earth in place, and with all of the new vegetation stripped away due to the drought, the winds of the Dust Bowl blew away about 850 million tons of topsoil in 1935 alone according to several estimates.

It is thought that if farmers and landowners had used better practices of agriculture and land stewardship, the Dust Bowl wouldn't have wreaked as much widespread devastation during the 1930s. Had the Israelites never turned from the ways of the Lord, their own agricultural disaster might have been averted as well. We have since recovered from the great losses of the Dust Bowl and history has shown us that fertility was restored to the land of Israel. But Joel also holds forth a vision of a time when God's spirit will pour among the people and sons and daughters will speak new truths (Joel 2:28). Before we allow our own soils to wither and diminish under our watch, we are challenged by Joel's words to reflect and ask whether our practices are causing joy to fade from the earth and its people (Joel 1:12) or if it is time for a new vision.

The complicated reality is that conventional farming has saved lives. My home of Des Moines, Iowa, is home to the World Food Prize, which celebrates the contributions of Norman Borlaug. Borlaug experienced the Dust Bowl and believed the solution was more technology. So he developed strains of wheat and rice that have saved a billion lives from starvation across the world. Monoculture—growing only one crop at a time or only one crop in a field—has drastically increased the yields of those grains. My dad is a conventional farmer. My brothers both work for John Deere, which manufactures the machines needed for such operations. Lives have been saved and economies thrive based upon the methods of conventional farming.

However, we strip the soil of its natural fertility in the process, and we have to depend upon chemicals to make this growth possible. It is a vicious cycle, because the more chemicals you use, the less the soil is replenished, and the more chemicals you need. If instead, we practiced better responsibility and dominion over the land by rotating crops that help create natural fertility, we'd actually come out ahead in both nutrition and in production.

If you compared two fields of wheat, one organic and one conventional, you likely would harvest more wheat on the conventional field today. But a farmer who practices better land stewardship through cover crops and rotation is actually able to produce more food if you count all of the various grains harvested together. One organic wheat farmer featured in

Barber's book plants four crops on his fields each year: wheat, of course, but also other grains like cowpeas, barley, and oats to help replenish the soil's fertility.

It all depends upon what you seek to value. Do we value a variety of grains, which together help the soil to thrive? That is where everyday people like you and me who consume food can change the equation: by choosing to purchase grains like barley and oats, we can change the market demands so that farmers would have a financial incentive to practice better stewardship. There is naturally an abundance at our fingertips, if only we would learn to appreciate the incredible diversity the earth has to offer. The earth is longing to provide and produce; it is meant to be fertile and bear fruit. What God has provided us is a gift, and the variety of this planet's earth and mineral life should bring us joy.

The prophet Joel's command to the fertile land to rejoice and be glad comes on the heels of the repentance of the people. We have been called to practice dominion, to be responsible for this earth. So let us till and keep this planet in way that fosters diversity and growth. Let us farm the land in a way that appreciates what it has to offer instead of forcing our way and our preferences upon it. Let us grow nature and help the land become more healthy day by day. Let us rejoice and celebrate and be grateful for every gift of grain and speck of soil. If we do, God promises that there will be abundance and plenty and the fertile land will have reason to rejoice.

This year, as I gather with my mom and my aunts to once again bake the treats that will fill our holiday tables, I'm hoping to experiment with a few new recipes. I want to invest in a grain mill so I can take some of the whole kernels of grain from the abundance that God has provided and truly appreciate the flavor and nutritional value. I'm curious about how oat flour might taste in our Rolo cookies and whether the date pinwheel cookies will benefit from the use of some barley. I'm not afraid to let go of some family traditions in order to allow the blessings of the earth to become the blessings of our table.

Questions for Reflection and Discussion

1. Isaiah paints for us a picture of a joyful feast on the day of salvation. What does feasting look like in your family?

2. We have life because of the fertile soil. From it we were formed and it is the source of all of our food and nutrition. What did you learn about the soil in our reflection this week?

3. The magi paid attention to the skies and were led on a journey. If we pay attention to the weeds in our garden they might lead us in a different direction. What in nature is calling out for your attention?

4. What does it mean to have responsibility for the land in which we live? How can you embrace the call of God to practice dominion?

5. Sometimes we make decisions based upon what creates abundance today, instead of thinking about the long-term consequences or benefits of other choices. Name examples of where you have seen this in your life.

Prayer

Holy God, you have set before us abundant life, incredible resources, and fertile land. Yet, too often, we have transformed them for our convenience and stripped them of their plentitude. Help us, in this season of Advent, to receive these gifts sacramentally and with great joy, so that we might increase the abundance of the land. Amen.

Focus for the Week

Think about the holiday meal your family will experience this time of year and how you might increase the fertility of the land all around us through your choices.

- Consider offering dishes that celebrate the diversity of fruits, vegetables, and grains grown in your region.
- Think about ways to incorporate less common grains in your holiday baked goods.
- Abundance on the dinner table is always a blessing, but ease both your levels of stress and waste by not preparing too much food.
- Compost what you can from both your prep work and from the leftovers. And don't forget that things like egg shells and coffee grounds make great additions to any compost.

Chapter 4

THE PEACE OF THE WORLD

The wolf will live with the lamb,
*   and the leopard will lie down with the young goat;*
*   the calf and the young lion will feed together,*
*   and a little child will lead them.*
The cow and the bear will graze.
*   Their young will lie down together,*
*   and a lion will eat straw like an ox.*
A nursing child will play over the snake's hole;
*   toddlers will reach right over the serpent's den.*
They won't harm or destroy anywhere on my
holy mountain.

(Isaiah 11:6-9)

I heard about a pastor who wanted to focus on the real and down-to-earth aspects of the Christmas story and what it must have been like to gather around the manger. In order to set the scene for Christmas worship, he brought live animals and straw into the sanctuary and strategically placed manure around the church so that *all* of the senses might be engaged. The point was to make the church smell like a stable and to emphasize the lowly and difficult conditions in which our Savior was born.

As the traditions around the Nativity story tell us, Mary and Joseph arrive in Bethlehem late in the night and she is about to give birth any minute. They knock on doors and try all of the inns, but there is no room and no one will let them in. So they give up and take shelter in the barn, with only the animals for company. In the wee hours of the night, Jesus is born, among the sheep and cattle, the straw and... well, whatever the animals have left behind.

From "Away in the Manger" to "The First Noel," "The Little Drummer Boy" to "While Shepherds Watched Their Flocks by Night," our Advent and Christmas hymns are filled with images of gentle beasts gathering around the manger and doing their part to welcome the Christ Child. One of my favorites is "The Friendly Beasts," in which the various animals each take a verse to share about "the gift he gave Immanuel." It's easy to romanticize the presence of animal life around the birth of Jesus. But we must not miss the way this points to the hope Jesus brings for all creation, including the animals. The animals receive Jesus' birth as good news, and they respond with peace.

A few years back, some photos began circulating on the Internet of a Nativity scene in a town square in Criciuma, Brazil. The scene includes life-sized statues of a donkey and an ox, along with an angel, kings, and of course Mary and Joseph. But there was an unexpected addition. A puppy, part German Shepherd and part mutt, was curled up in the manger with Jesus. It is likely that the dog was a stray that had no idea what the figures in that scene meant but had simply found a warm, soft place to sleep.

Isn't that exactly what all of creation waits for? Isn't that the vision of the peaceable kingdom Isaiah spoke about? It is a place of safety and rest, of plenty and companionship; a world where leopards and goats, stray dogs and sleeping babies lie down together without fear. As we have been reflecting during this Advent season about the coming kingdom of God, we remember that the creatures of the land, sky, and sea are waiting, too.

Man's Best Friend

In the modern, Western worldview there is typically a separation between animal and human lives, even among farmers. Even though I grew up on a farm, my dad focused on cultivating grains and not raising livestock. We had a few goats when I was very little and dogs that roamed wherever they wanted, but we never had pets that were allowed in the house. I would visit the cattle, hogs, and chickens at my grandparents' farm, but they didn't eat and sleep in the house with us.

And that is true for most of us. We have very little personal connection with the birds of the air, the fish of the sea, or the creatures of the land until we go to the grocery store and purchase perfectly portioned packages of meat. When we get the spiral cut ham out of the freezer and stick it in the roasting pan, we do so with very little appreciation for the hog whose life was given so that we might share in a Christmas feast.

Our relationship with the animal life of this world was intended to be very different.

As the days of Creation proceed in the first chapter of Genesis, God commands the waters and the sky and the land to be filled with living creatures (Genesis 1:20-25). And then in the middle of the sixth day, God shifts attention to the creation of humanity. Humans are made "in God's own image," so that we might "take charge of the fish of the sea, the birds in the sky, the livestock, all the earth, and all the crawling things on earth" (Genesis 1:26-27). We are unique creatures created for a special relationship with God and given a relationship of responsibility with the rest of creation.

I recently discovered a sermon of John Wesley, the founder of the Methodist tradition, called "The General Deliverance." In it, Wesley explores God's intentions for "the brute creation," as he calls the animals, from their original state in creation to their place in the new creation. As he describes the relationship between humanity and the "inferior creatures" in the garden, Wesley believed that each was created with will and understanding and freedom, but humanity bore the image of God. And so we alone out of all the creation were capable of knowing, loving, and obeying God. Because of this, "man was the channel of conveyance between his Creator and the whole brute creation."[1] And just as the fulfillment of our purpose was to love and obey God, so was it the fulfillment of the creatures to love and obey humanity.

Not only have we failed to love and care for the "brute creation," but we have failed to care for one another. Isaiah recounts various ways we have rejected the image of God in our fellow human beings and "why the LORD's anger burned against the people" (Isaiah 5:8-25). But he also receives a vision that challenges us to set aside our violence and wickedness (Isaiah

11:4) and to reclaim the kinds of relationships God intended. When Isaiah extends that vision to the animals in Isaiah 11:6-9, he is reminding us that God's intention has always been that our care for one another spills over to bless the rest of creation.

As *The New Interpreter's Bible* notes, the command to take charge in Genesis 1:28, to *have dominion* (NRSV), "reveals that it must be understood in terms of care-giving, even nurturing, not exploitation...human beings should relate to the nonhuman as God relates to them."[2] This relationship between human and animal life is expanded in Genesis 2 where a human is formed first. However, God does not think it is good for this creature to be alone. So God desires to make a helper and forms other living beings: the animals. But "a helper perfect for him was nowhere to be found" until "with the rib taken from the human, the LORD God fashioned a woman" (Genesis 2:20, 22).

The animals of the world were meant to be our companions, to exist alongside us, and even if they are not our perfect helpers, they are our responsibility. The picture painted in Isaiah 11 of the coming kingdom of God could just as easily have described the harmony in the garden in Genesis. When we imagine a little child leading (Isaiah 11:6), a nursing child and toddler playing right in the midst of what we think of as fierce predators (Isaiah 11:8), we feel deep in our bones the love of God's presence permeating all relationships.

I think we catch a glimpse of that peaceable kingdom of Isaiah in the way many human families welcome pets into their lives. On our very first Christmas together, my husband and I adopted a kitten. Turbo was our first baby and from the time he was little, he has always wanted to curl up in a ball next to a warm body. To this day, when we go to bed, he flops down on the pillow next to me with his head resting on my shoulder. Our second cat, Tiki, is a fat orange creature that looks a lot like Garfield. He is incredibly lazy and will not play with any toys, unless you get out a string; then he goes wild. He is willing to cuddle only on his own terms—usually by lying on your feet or somewhere just past arm's reach. When he does decide to get close, however, he will lie on your chest; all twenty-four pounds of cat will purr loudly enough to keep you awake.

Because I didn't grow up with pets in my home, falling in love with these two creatures has been a new experience for me. I don't think that I ever really appreciated the personalities, love, or companionship of animals until they became a part of our lives. And when I think about what it might mean to practice dominion, as God has called us to, I think about the immense responsibility to care for these two creatures, to provide for them, to share my home and to help them thrive. Even when that means getting down on hands and knees in servant love to clean out the litter box.

Keeping these two cats as pets has helped me understand dominion in a new way. In my experience of the love and companionship of these domesticated creatures, I also recognize the cosmic, far-reaching implications of Isaiah's vision of the peaceable kingdom in Isaiah 11:6-9. God intends to restore peace in all relationships between created beings.

The Food Chain

Too often, violence marks those relationships instead. Commenting on the close of the first two chapters in Genesis, biblical scholar Terence Fretheim notes that "the future stands genuinely open here. All depends on what the human does with what God presents…human judgment will shape the nature of the next divine decision, indeed the future of the world."[3] But as we have explored already, humanity gets it wrong. Our hearts turned inward toward ourselves and we rebelled against God, and the "next divine decision" was to cut us off from the abundant life of the garden.

Wesley writes about the impact this had on the brute creatures and how "the very foundations of their nature are out of course"[4] as a result. Although formed initially to be our helpers and companions, no longer do the creatures love and obey humanity; now they flee from us or would seek to destroy us. All living creatures, including humanity, were initially given by God plant life for food. To humans God gave plants yielding seeds and the fruits of trees, and to the wildlife God gave "all the green grasses for food" (Genesis 1:29-30). The entire world was vegetarian. All created beings were meant to live in peaceful relationship, rather than as links in a food chain. With humanity's failure in the garden, however, those relationships became torn. Now we live in a world where some animals kill and consume others for their food.

Just as our hearts are caught up in violence and destruction, so, too, the animals turn and destroy one another. Observing the natural order of things around him, Wesley notes that "an immense majority of creatures, perhaps a million to one, can no otherwise preserve their own lives, than by destroying their fellow-creatures!"[5] Leopards and wolves eat goats and lambs; lions and bears devour cattle; poisonous snakes bite humans, even small children.

During my Organic Ministry class in 2015, I spent an entire day each month on my friend Tim Diebel's farm, Taproot Garden. There was time for reflection on our readings, work on the land, conversation about ministry, and also time for Sabbath. One of my favorite things to do during that unstructured hour was to sit by the chickens and simply watch them interact and strut around the yard. While they appear on the surface to be such gentle, beautiful creatures, the reality is that they are part of a violent circle of life. When you watch them there in the yard, you soon see that they peck and scratch and will rip apart any worm or bug that crosses their path. As John Wesley notes, it isn't just the large creatures of prey that destroy other lives; even the "innocent songsters of the grove" eat forms of life that are lower on the food chain than themselves.[6]

Of course, most of us don't get so attached to insects that we grieve their loss. Or even the loss of chickens for that matter. But as Tim and his wife, Lori, have gradually grown their flock, they have grown to care a great deal for those birds. Tim calls them "the girls," and he lets them out of the coop every morning, pampers them with great feed and treats from the garden, gathers their eggs, and safely tucks them in every night. Occasionally the chickens get territorial, and sometimes bigger ones will pick on the smaller ones. So Tim has established multiple coops and a process for integrating new birds into the flock to help manage those realities. But you can't guard against every danger, and you can't change the fact that chickens are also prey.

My heart broke one afternoon as I saw a post from Tim on his blog about "nature's harder edge." Just as he was heading out to put the girls to bed for the night, there was a commotion in the yard. The chickens were in chaos and making a ruckus, and Tim caught out of the corner of his eye something larger that had been scared away by his presence. When he finally had a chance to take in the scene, he discovered three dead hens. The commotion had been caused by foxes, who had been watching for just the right moment to grab dinner.

In the midst of his grief, Tim's words capture the tension of what it means to live in this time of longing for the new creation. "Here in the rawness of God's order are pests and diseases in the garden and thieving birds and squirrels in the orchard. There are moles tunneling through the yard, and there are predators above and around the chicken yard attentively watching for and eventually seizing their hungry opportunity. It's beautiful out here, and serene, but it's also torn feathers and blood, rot and thorn."[7]

Isaiah holds before us a vision of the day when none will "harm or destroy anywhere on my holy mountain" (Isaiah 11:9). But this promise of animals living in harmony, predator and prey dwelling together without violence, remains unfulfilled. The reality of torn feathers and blood—pain and violence, death and destruction—amplifies our longing for the day when the lion and the leopard will return to diets of grass and straw, and will graze alongside the ones who would have been their meals (Isaiah 11:6-7).

Corn-Fed Confinement

In the initial vision of Creation, we have a glimpse of the peaceable kingdom Isaiah foretold. All creatures feasted on the grasses of the earth instead of one another. But the actions of humanity impacted the natural order of God's world; sin, death, and decay became our reality. The world became so infested with violence and corruption that God essentially started over, flooding the earth and saving but a few humans and creatures (Genesis 6–9).

Yet despite Noah's righteousness, he is still a human being and therefore flawed because of the first humans' sin. Speaking after the Flood, God recognizes that "the ideas of the human mind are evil from their youth" (Genesis 8:21). Terence Fretheim notes that "although Noah is in some sense a new Adam, God's moves into the future must now take into account the evil inclination of the human heart....The post-flood world is no Garden of Eden."[8] And so the rules change as a result of the new natural order: humans may now eat animals.

In Genesis 9:1-5, God allows humanity to consider all living and moving creatures as part of their new food supply...with a caveat. All of creation is still a gift, and God still desires life even in the midst of our tendency toward destruction. So the taking of every life is serious, and the symbol of that gift is the blood of all creatures. Blood must not be consumed (Genesis 9:4). As Fretheim explains, although animals are given to the human beings for food, this is "not a license for exploitation nor a diminution in the task of dominion."[9] We are still responsible for how we care for all creatures and the proscription of Genesis 9:4 is one way to guard against needlessly harming animals, whether through cruelty or simple carelessness. Today, as we live into Isaiah's vision of peace we should take seriously the spirit of God's commandment to Noah—to regard and care for the lives of animals...including those we eat for food.

Now, I love a good steak, or roasted chicken, or bacon... wow, do I love bacon. But I also grew up near small farms, and so I know what the possibility is for raising those animals in ethical and humane ways. I've experienced what it's like to take care for their lives. I can remember a time when we had to bring a calf into the house that had been born too early that spring. The ground was still cold and frozen, and it was pretty sick. My uncle had wrapped it up in blankets and brought it inside. We gave that calf a warm bath in the tub. When it was all dried off, that calf was the fluffiest and softest cow I had ever met. We made up bottles of formula, and I can still remember straining to hold on to that gigantic bottle while the calf sucked and fed and nearly pulled it away from me. You had to get in really close, holding the calf's head in place with one arm and juggling the bottle with the other. All the while, you couldn't help but just stare into those big, beautiful eyes.

Unfortunately, today many of us are so far removed from these creatures that we neither appreciate their lives nor do we care how our supper gets on the table. Last week, we explored the mass production of food from the perspective of the soil and grains, but we have also pushed past the boundaries of our dominion when it comes to our consumption of meat. Many industrial confinement operations today treat these animals in ways that no human being would ever want to be treated.

A great example of this, lifted up by Dan Barber in his book *The Third Plate*, is poultry. Chickens, like my friend Tim raises, are actually omnivores; they will eat small bugs and insects as well as grains and grasses. For ages in this country, almost every farmer had chickens. They could raise enough to eat and maybe a few to sell. But in the 1920s and 30s, the chicken began to be transformed. Farmers began to raise them in huge numbers, with the unstated goal of converting their feed grain into chicken meat as efficiently and cheaply as possible. While chickens would prefer to roam, we locked them up in small cages and radically limited their diet by only feeding them corn. This process will pack on the calories for these poultry, in part because we do the foraging for them, but it also reduces the vitamins and minerals present in the finished meat. And we do the same with other livestock, too. This is a far cry from Isaiah's vision of calf and lion, cow and bear feeding together—predator and prey alike receiving without cruelty or violence the nourishment they need to thrive.

Yet as Barber points out, some people like the renowned chef Jean-Louis Palladin resisted this tendency—not because it was cruel or harmful, but because the resulting meat was a lower quality for food. The taste and nutrients just weren't there anymore. In essence, we have taken the good gifts of God, the gifts given to us even in the midst of our sin and rebellion, and we mistreat and misuse them and lose out both in our relationship with these amazing creatures and in their flavor and nutritional benefits as food.

The harmony of all life proclaimed in our passage from Isaiah must begin with us, with humans seeking a better relationship with animals. As much as Wesley reflected upon the violence within the created order, he also lamented the way the brute creation is "exposed to the violence and cruelty of him that is now their common enemy—man…the human shark, without any such necessity, torments them of his free choice."[10] And so, he preached on the longing of brute creatures to be delivered from the bondage of this corruption. Not only did he believe that in the new creation they would be restored to full and abundant life, but that God's creatures would be repaid for their sufferings in the present as well. He encouraged people to remember God's care for every inferior creature in the hope that it would soften our hearts toward them here and now.

The Shepherd King

Our ideas of God's redemption of the world often don't take enough account of the restoration of all creation, including animal life, in God's kingdom. Elizabeth Johnson wrote a great piece for *U.S. Catholic* about how God so loved the world, the whole cosmos, all of creation. She tells in it the story of a naturalist by the name of John Muir, who came across a dead bear in Yosemite and criticized those who "make no room in heaven for such noble creatures: 'Not content with taking all of Earth, they also claim the celestial country as the only ones who possess the kinds of souls for which that imponderable empire was planned.' To the contrary, Muir believed, God's 'charity is broad enough for bears' "[11]

I was about seven years old when the movie *All Dogs Go to Heaven* came out. I remember watching it often when I was that age, but had mostly forgotten the plot until I started thinking about John Muir, the peaceable kingdom, and a heaven filled with bears. The movie itself actually epitomizes the violence and destruction of our human hearts; we are distracted by greed, use others for our own profit, and seek revenge wherever we can. It is only at the end, when Charlie gives his life in order to save another, that the rascally dog earns back his place in heaven. The redemption of all creatures points to the fullest redemption of humankind as well.

Wesley was not alone in advocating for humans to treat creatures with more dignity and love. Charles Spurgeon once wrote, "It is not only for the sake of the creature subject to cruelty that we would plead for kindness, but with a view to the good of the person causing the pain; for cruelty hardens the heart, deadens the conscience, and destroys the finer sensibilities of the soul.... for the man who truly loves his Maker becomes tender towards all the creatures his Lord has made."[12] Treating the whole of creation with kindness is evidence that humans ourselves are being transformed into creatures who love.

And so we cannot divorce Isaiah's vision of the peaceable kingdom in our focus text for this week from the verses that precede it. Isaiah 11 begins with a promise of righteousness for those who suffer. In verses 1-5, we hear good news of hope for all who are needy and oppressed. And in our text, verses 6-9, that good news becomes a message of peace even among animals. The promised one will come to transform all relationships, human or otherwise. As Gene Tucker notes, "the rule of justice in human society is followed or paralleled by a transformation in the relationship among animals and between animals and human beings."[13] When our hearts are right, peace will prevail for all creatures.

And God calls us to account. In these days of Advent, we are comforted by the image of peaceful animals around the manger. We hear the good news shared with the shepherds and sheep in the fields of Bethlehem. But the expectation of Advent is not only about preparing our hearts for the birth of Jesus, but for

Christ to come once again. We are waiting for God's kingdom to burst forth and set us free from the endless cycle of violence and death, revenge and pain. The peaceful animals around the manger are a foretaste, but we are still waiting. We are waiting for that day of endless peace, justice, and righteousness for all creatures.

Isaiah reminds us that our Savior will come to judge with wisdom and strength (Isaiah 11:2-4), and I am reminded of the vision of the King of kings on the throne given to us by Matthew. We are told that when the Human One comes there will be a reckoning and that "all the nations will be gathered in front of him. He will separate them from each other, just as a shepherd separates the sheep from the goats" (Matthew 25:32).

Though the shepherd is a biblical metaphor for royalty, historically speaking shepherds and kings belong on opposite ends of the social spectrum. While kings have armies at their disposal, the shepherd personally protects the sheep; his very body is their first line of defense. While a king leads from on high, issuing orders through his commanders and sending word through the land, the shepherd leads from the midst of the sheep. Kings are often indifferent to the plight of their people, but a shepherd knows each one in his flock by name. And a shepherd wouldn't hesitate to leave behind the entire flock in order to search for one that was lost.

Jesus, the Prince of Peace, judges us and will call us to account in the way such a shepherd would. He will gather the flock together and call them by name. He will speak, and at the sound of his voice those who recognize him will come running near. And even as we identify with the sheep, we are reminded in this

Scripture that we are supposed to do likewise. We respond to Isaiah's prophecy of a righteous judge, a shoot from the stump of Jesse, by reaching out to the least and the last and the lost. We are called to turn our hearts toward all, human and otherwise, in love and care and responsibility.

God has never stopped calling us to practice dominion responsibly and care for all of the creatures of this world. When we do so, we usher in that peaceable kingdom in our corner of the world until that day comes when God restores the face of the earth. On that day, in John Wesley's words, all creatures "will be delivered from all irregular appetites.... No rage will be found in any creature, no fierceness, no cruelty, or thirst for blood."[14] It is the hope embodied in the words of Isaiah, that "the calf and the young lion will feed together, / and a little child will lead them" (Isaiah 11: 6). All the earth is waiting for Christ to come again as the Prince of Peace and Shepherd King.

Questions for Reflection and Discussion

1. Animals are such an important part of our Christmas hymnody. What is your favorite Christmas hymn featuring God's creatures and why?

2. How have you experienced the love of a pet or an animal? In what way are animals companions to human beings? In what ways are the "brute creatures" unsatisfactory helpers?

3. Some people choose a vegetarian diet as an expression of their faith. In Scripture, we are reminded that God did give us all creatures for food, but encouraged us

to honor their life in the process. How does your faith inform your eating habits?

4. John Wesley names the violence of the food chain but sees humanity as the worst predator of them all because we kill or harm without necessity. What are ways you can work to prevent the cruel treatment of animals by others?

5. What does it mean to you that God loves us like shepherds care for their sheep? How does that inform how we should shepherd the creatures of this world?

Prayer

Holy God, you formed us in your image and called us to honor the life in every created being. We are grateful for the company of the creatures and for the sustenance they bring. Forgive us for when we have considered our neighbors, whether human, fish, fowl, or critter, to be less than one of your holy creations. Help us, O God, in this season of Advent, to be tender to all living beings and to live into the peaceable kingdom. Amen.

Focus for the Week

Christmas is the season of giving, but many have more than they need or want. When purchasing items, you can look for leather, wool, or wool products that are ethically produced or products that are not tested on animals. You might also think about how you might use this time of year to bless organizations that work with the animals of the world.

- Collect items for local veterinary offices and animal shelters like old towels, pet food, newspapers, and cleaning supplies like dish soap and bleach.
- Make a monetary donation to a program that brings therapy animals to nursing homes or hospitals or a local nature center that promotes education with children.
- Give the gift of animals by supporting the work of organizations like Heifer International that empower small-scale farmers across the world through training and livestock.
- Consider adopting a rescue animal and giving it a home in your home.

Chapter 5

GOD MOVES INTO THE NEIGHBORHOOD

*This is what God planned for the climax of all
times: to bring all things together in Christ, the
things in heaven along with the things on earth.*
(Ephesians 1:10)

We have spent so much time during this season of Advent exploring the two Creation stories in Genesis, but there is a third Creation story that is very dear to my heart. Every Christmas Eve in my congregation, we turn to the first chapter of the Gospel of John and hear another telling of how this world was made (John 1:1-14).

"In the beginning was the Word....Everything came into being through the Word..." (John 1:1-3).

As we prepare our hearts to hear that Gospel reading, we turn the overhead lights down low and sit for a moment with only the Advent and Christ candles to give us light. Then, quietly and gently, the familiar notes of "Silent Night" start to play. A single taper is lit, and the light of Christ is passed throughout the church.

For the past few years, the flame that we share with one another has had a really special significance because it comes from Bethlehem... literally. In the Church of the Nativity in Bethlehem, built on the traditional site where Jesus is said to have been born, there is a continuous flame that has burned for centuries. Each year, a child helps deliver the light to Vienna. Delegations from across Europe carry the flame across the continent and one lamp is sent to New York City, where it then is distributed across the United States. The flame from the grotto is carried across the world as a sign of peace.*

One of our local agencies hosts this "Peace Light" each December, so a few days before Christmas Eve we drive over with a small oil lamp safely tucked in a box and receive the flame. Various people are responsible for keeping the lamp burning until it is finally time to worship. And then, as our services begin on that holy night, we light the Christ candle from the lamp.

At the end of worship, as we pass the flame, we sing together of the "Son of God, love's pure light." By the end of the song, the entire sanctuary is aglow with the light of Christ and we open the Gospel of John and read from the first chapter:

> *What came into being*
> *through the Word was life,*
> *and the life was the light for all people....*

---

* You can find out more details or discover if the "Peace Light" will be near you at www.peacelight.org.

The Word became flesh
  and made his home among us.
We have seen his glory . . ."

                                          (John 1:3-4, 14)

If all earth is waiting, this is what it is waiting for. It is the reconciliation of heaven and earth. As Gail O'Day reminds us in *The New Interpreter's Bible* (Vol. IX), these opening words in John's Gospel set the stage for all that will come after; this is the story of the heavens and earth. We often focus on two separate realms of God's presence: that cosmic reality where the Word created all things and the temporal, earthly reality into which Jesus was born. But what we discover in our journey of faith is that these are not disjointed and disconnected realities. In the beginning, God created both the heavens and the earth (Genesis 1:1). In the end of our story, it is a new heaven and a new earth that will replace what had existed (Revelation 21:1). In the life of Jesus Christ, the heavens and earth are brought together and opened up to the presence of God. The Word of God took on our created life and "made his home among us" (John 1:14), or as *THE MESSAGE* translation puts it, God "moved into the neighborhood."

I think about how God moved into the neighborhood as I look around at the faces of all of those who are gathered in my church on Christmas Eve. Standing at the front, I can look them each in the eye and I can see reflected in their faces the light of that flame from Bethlehem. It is one of those "thin places" where the boundary between heaven and earth seems to melt away. God really is present, and it is a powerful experience.

God Has a Plan

As John's Gospel reminds us, everything comes from God and is destined for light and life. Nothing in this world can stop that from being true. The good news we hear in the midst of all of our waiting and longing and expectation is that God has a plan. In the Letter to the Ephesians, we are reminded that at "the climax of all times," God will bring the heavens and earth together in Christ. How God will do so is the focus of our key Scripture for this Christmas.

"Before the creation of the world," Ephesians tells us, God had a plan and that plan was Jesus Christ (Ephesians 1:4-5).

Before the star led the magi to Bethlehem.

Before the prophets heard God's voice.

Before the moon or the stars were set in the sky.

Before everything, while "the earth was without shape or form" (Genesis 1:2), while "the Word was with God and the Word was God," (John 1:1) there was a plan that God set into motion. And that plan included and involved the whole grand epic of human faith.

What kind of plan is this? If we look to the root of the word that is used here in Ephesians, *oikonomia*, we find that it refers to the administration of a household or an estate. It's the same word that is the source of our words *ecology* and *economy*, how systems hold together and function. It also refers to the idea of stewardship and management and caretaking. The use of this word implies that the heavens and the earth are held together in God's household. And so from the very beginning, God's plan and intent for all of creation, the rules set forth in stewardship and care and love, has been that the heavens and earth would be brought together within God's household through Christ.

Sabbath Rest

When we go back to explore again the first Creation story of Genesis, we can see the blueprints of this plan. In Genesis 1:1, God sets about to create "the heavens and the earth," not separately, but as if it were one creation. As the narrative concludes, we are reminded that all of the work of creation includes "the heavens and the earth and all who live in them" (Genesis 2:1). When the work was done and the plans were laid, God rested (Genesis 2:2).

When my work is finished, I like to rest, too. One of my guilty pleasures during my free time is to binge-watch television shows. I have a variety of things I watch and sometime ago I got hooked on the show *Supernatural*. The premise includes these two young men, the Winchesters, who chase after monsters and save people's lives. The twists and turns of the plot have them interacting with angels and demons and all sorts of spiritual beings. As a pastor, I find it fascinating how the secular culture of today appropriates religious ideas and where they get it "right" and "wrong." In this particular show, almost all of the characters know God exists, but the Ruler of Heaven is nowhere to be found. Sometime after the world was created, God took a vacation and hasn't returned.

This idea of an absent God resonates with many in our world today. There are some in this world who view God in a hands-off sort of way. They might believe that God had a plan and created the world, but it's all set in stone now and so there is nothing for

God to do. Others find God distant, hidden, and wonder if maybe God has stopped speaking...or at least has stopped speaking to them. Still others might look around and seeing little evidence of the goodness of creation, they imagine that God has skipped town and left us to fend for ourselves.

Our Scriptures, however, consistently remind us of God's presence. As we lift up every time we celebrate Christ's birth, "The Word became flesh / and made his home among us" (John 1:14). As the psalmist cries out, "Where could I go to get away from your spirit? / Where could I go to escape your presence?" (Psalm 139:7). As the Israelites escaped Egypt, the Lord personally led them through columns of cloud and lightning (Exodus 13:21). And that desire of God to dwell in the presence of the heavens and the earth is the foundation of the Sabbath rest of Genesis 2:2-3. Yet, just as we often forget the promises of God's presence, we have often misunderstood the blessings of Sabbath.

Genesis tells us that the Sabbath is the day when God rests, but I know I have often associated that rest with separation. God finished the work and then "blessed the seventh day and made it holy" (Genesis 2:3). We imagine that after doing all the work of building, creating, and giving life, God took a day off, apart from the heavens and the earth. We hear that holiness echoed in the command of Exodus 20:8-11 to "remember the Sabbath day and treat it as holy." In Hebrew, the verb for holy is *qadash*, which can be translated as "set apart."

So the Sabbath, and with it God's presence, God's kingdom, becomes something distant or separate from the world we inhabit for the other six days of the week. We come to think that the creation is simply our temporary home, and we use up all of these amazing gifts thinking that our ultimate purpose is to get to where God is: the kingdom of God. And because we are always trying to get to this holy, set-apart reality, we see this fulfillment as outside of our current experience. Wayne Muller, author of *Sabbath: Finding Rest, Renewal, and Delight in Our Busy Lives*, thinks we therefore find reasons to "despoil our nest, we ruin our air and soil, because it is all dispensable, we will not be here long, because here is no good, it is not where we are going."[1]

But theologian Jürgen Moltmann understands the Sabbath in a very different way, as "the day when God is present."[2] The other acts of creation are works and actions that express God's will, he writes, but when God rests—when God stops all that activity—God is in our midst and we finally understand who God is. God has created this world, with its elements and plants and cosmos and people, not for the sake of creating and then stepping away, but for the sake of being in relationship; for the sake of the Sabbath. The Gospel of John talks about God making a home among us, and in this Sabbath rest that is exactly what God does. God finishes the creation by creating Sabbath and resting among us.

As the seasons of *Supernatural* have progressed, the Winchesters discover that there are books being written about them and track down the author. They think that he is a prophet of God, but in a really interesting twist (spoiler alert), it turns out that the author, Chuck Edlund, was actually God. And this God didn't want to sit back and watch creation happen, but wanted to experience it. When asked about why he was walking around on earth with all of the people, he says he likes front-row seats, so he decided to hide out in plain sight. And so, God (in *Supernatural*) wrote himself into the storyline. God didn't separate from the world, but was hidden precisely because he had entered into the world so completely.

In the same way, our story of faith tells us that God doesn't retreat but dives deep into our lives. The holiness of Sabbath isn't about separation, but about sacred connection. Moltmann writes that God rests and "begins to 'experience' the beings he has created...he allows himself to be affected, to be touched by each of his creatures. He adopts the community of creation.... He allows them to exist in his presence. And he is present in their existence."[3] The Sabbath is a time of appreciation and joy. It is a time of hoping and longing, dreaming and imagining. In this act of completion, God sets all of creation free to be what we will be.

And when you think about it that way, the Sabbath of God is the plan set in motion before the creation of the earth. God creates us and on this day of rest and presence, heaven and earth are one. This is what God's household looks like; this is the economy of love and the ecology of grace. We are told to honor the Sabbath and to keep it holy, because whenever we stop and rest in God's presence, we are experiencing that plan of God. As Wayne Muller reminds us, Jesus encouraged Sabbath practice: "*Make your home in me*, he said, *as I make mine in you.* The kingdom is within you, he reminded them, alive and miraculous this very moment."[4] On this day, we can cease our endless striving and making and doing. We simply get to enjoy and find peace in the presence of God, to experience the oneness of heaven and earth.

I must admit that I rarely see or practice Sabbath in this way. I am always rushing here and there, from a meeting to a project, to home and back. My life is constantly busy with the work of the church, and my family, and making dinner, and doing laundry. When I finally get to the small bit of downtime that I have set aside for myself, I usually "veg out" in front of the television and watch things like *Supernatural*. I check out of the world, much like I thought God had on the Sabbath.

Occasionally, however, I find an opportunity to dive deeper and open myself to all that is around me. I have found that when I go outside and connect with nature as a part of that practice, I'm finally able to stop the wheels in my head from turning. I can simply be. I find that my ego is diminished. And I am humbly reminded of all the amazing things happening in the world without me: The falling of snowflakes. The squirrels playing in the trees. The hawk gliding overhead. The slow decomposition of leaves that are life and death all wrapped into one. I am overcome by how small I am and how beautiful the world is.

The gift of Sabbath is a glimpse of the kingdom of God we long for. Every time we rest in the presence of God, we enter God's life; we taste eternity; we experience heaven and earth being brought together. On the flip side, without stopping to pause and connect with this world around us and the Creator of all there is, we forget who we are.

Maybe God's mysterious plan from Ephesians is, at least initially, the Sabbath, when God rests in the presence and company of all of creation. As we have explored throughout this season of Advent and now Christmas, a huge part of that plan had to do with you and me. We were created in the image of

God and invited to practice dominion, to be responsible for this world. But God also leaves room for us to be what we will be, to respond how we will. We could choose to partner together with God to encourage growth and life and rest in God's Sabbath presence. Or, we could choose to turn from those gifts.

Wayne Muller believes that we often neglect the rest and joy of the Sabbath for things that "at first may seem expedient, or important, or profitable—but in the end they will bring you suffering.... You will become brittle and hard, and lose precious nourishment and joy."[5] We have explored this sentiment all throughout this study: How we reached for the fruit in the garden (Genesis 3:6-7) and found ourselves cast away from the abundance of life. How we have become caught in consumer impulses that waste resources and leave heaps of garbage in their wake. How we have stripped the fertility of the soil for harvests of abundance, creating nutrient-starved food in the process. How we now live in fear rather than peace because our call to love and protect all created beings was sacrificed on the altar of jealousy. Our response to God has been to strive for other things, to seek our own way, and in our sin we have backed away from God. We have separated heaven and earth.

God with Us

The arc of Scriptures, the hope of our faith, lies in the assertion of John that "the light shines in the darkness, / and the darkness doesn't extinguish the light" (John 1:5). We can turn our backs on God all we want and choose the darkness. We can seek our will and not God's will. We can make mistakes and fail in our humble striving. But God is not content to be driven out of our lives. God refuses to be turned away. Instead, God chooses to act over and over again in ways that bring heaven and earth back together. In Joseph Sittler's words, our God "drives, loves, and suffers his world towards restoration...that the whole cosmos in its brokenness...might be restored to wholeness, joy, and...love."[6]

And so God heard the cries of the oppressed in Egypt and rescued them and brought them into the land of milk and honey.

And so God called the people of faith over and over again through the words and actions of the prophets.

And so God chose finally to act, once and for all, by entering our lives.

In *Let Your Life Speak*, Parker Palmer tells this story about how he took an Outward Bound course to get a different perspective on his life. One of the experiences of his week on the coast of Maine was to rappel down a cliff. He was terrified and hesitant and he couldn't figure out how to do it. But the instructor kept working with him, and pretty soon he found a rhythm and was making his way—until an obstacle presented itself. Palmer froze, right there on the cliff face. That is, until he heard the words that got him to keep going: "If you can't get out of it, get into it." Palmer realized then that no alternative solution was going to present itself. The instructor wouldn't pull him up, and he wouldn't just magically float to the ground. Palmer writes that "I had long believed in the concept of 'the word become flesh' but until that moment I had not experienced it.... There was no way out of my dilemma except to get into it—so my feet started to move."[7]

Our God does not reject the brokenness of this world, and God refuses to destroy it again (Genesis 9). Instead of keeping distant or getting out of it, God gets into it, gets really close and dives deep into all of the mess and struggle, the pain and sorrow of our human and worldly lives. Maybe the rest of the Sabbath was God's first plan for holding together heaven and earth, but as we moved away from God, God chose a different tactic: God now moves toward us. The Word became flesh and took on our vulnerability and temptation, our frailty, and eventually, even our death.

And it happened with a particular life, in a particular time, in a particular place.

In the city of Bethlehem, to parents who really weren't anyone important, God was born. And as we read in the Scriptures, Mary "wrapped him snugly, and laid him in a manger, because there was no place for them in the guestroom" (Luke 2:7). In the Common English Bible, one of the things I notice right away is that it doesn't say that there was no place in the inn. It says guestroom, which is a fair translation of the Greek.

While the Greek word used here, *katalyma*, could be an inn where travelers spend a night, it could also refer to the sleeping area or guest space in the kind of single-room home most people lived in at that time in Judea. Many of the homes of Bethlehem would have consisted of one large living space, possibly with a smaller private room that might have been set aside for guests. In a traditional first-century home, there would have been an area where the animals were brought in at night to keep them safe. The large living space would often include mangers, typically built out of stone or hollowed out in the ground, where the straw for animals were kept.

With that sort of dwelling space in mind, when we read that there was "no place for them in the guestroom" (Luke 2:7), it may mean that the guestroom was already occupied or that there physically wasn't enough room for the birth. A better understanding of the text invites us to imagine Mary and Joseph surrounded by family, perhaps a bit too crowded by relatives, as Jesus is born.

On the one hand, it pains me to think that we often take this story out of context. I love the traditional story. I love that God shows up on the margins. I love preaching about how those mean innkeepers turned away the Holy Family, but how on Christmas Eve, we get to welcome God into our hearts.

But on the other hand, how amazing is the idea that Jesus was born in a normal home, surrounded by people and the animals that lived there. It wasn't far away from people and community, but right there, in the midst of an everyday life, that God moved into the neighborhood. Christ is born. Emmanuel. God with us.

The birth of Jesus Christ, the Word of God becoming flesh is the most significant event in the history of all creation, because the Incarnation fundamentally alters God's relationship to humankind and the world in which we live. This moment, this event, is so spectacular that it changes everything. God gets into our lives and speaks our words and breathes our air and tells stories and cooks us breakfast. And as Keith Innes says, the fact that God "became part of the ecosystem, has changed for all eternity the relation of earth to its Creator."[8]

And I think the most powerful statement of the Incarnation is the reminder that this earth, this creation, this is the site of our ultimate redemption. God's plan is not that this earth will waste away and we will be whisked away to heaven, but that in Jesus Christ all things, things in heaven and things on earth, will be brought together. Right here in our neighborhood is where God will bring us salvation. We can't get out of it. We cannot escape. The creation is a part of us. It sustains us. It is where we will be redeemed.

And if you can't get out of it, get into it.

A New Heaven and a New Earth

All throughout this study, we have been hearing about the new creation and the kingdom of God and this future potentiality. Advent is the time when we not only celebrate the Incarnation, the birth of Christ into our world, but we look ahead in expectation for that day when Christ will come again to bring all the earth into God's everlasting kingdom. It is the reminder that when the labor pains of this world cease a new creation will be born.

When Moltmann talks about this reality that we hope for and the longing of heaven and earth to be renewed, he calls it the kingdom of glory. When the triune God finally dwells among us, then "each created being in its own way...will participate in eternal life and in the eternal bliss of the God who is present among them."[9] Or in the words of Revelation, "death will be no more. There will be no mourning, crying, or pain anymore....There will no longer be any curse....Night will be no more. They won't need the light of a lamp or the light of the sun, for the Lord God will shine on them" (Revelation 21:4; 22:3, 5). At the climax of all times, the heavens and earth will be brought together and God will make a home among us.

We look around today and this is not yet our reality. We have been focusing simply on a few verses from Paul's Letter to the Ephesians, but if we read the whole epistle, we are reminded that the reconciliation we long for can be experienced, at least partially, right now. As Pheme Perkins writes in her commentary on Ephesians, "The mystery of bringing all things together in Christ may not yet be completed, but it has already become a reality in the church."[10]

From the moment the heavens opened and the angels began to proclaim the birth of our Messiah, we have been invited to participate and respond to the kingdom of glory. Moltmann writes that at this moment, "God's energies and potentialities appear in the visible world, in order to open the life systems which are closed in on themselves and to guide them into their new, richer future."[11] Shepherds leave their flocks and search out the baby in the manger. Magi travel great distances to greet the newborn King. Fishermen leave their boats to follow the Messiah. Rich men like Zacchaeus give away their wealth. And the ripples from the birth of that one moment built the church, the body of Christ alive in the world today.

Friends, you and I are that body of Christ and the presence of God dwells in our hearts. And as the Letter to the Ephesians goes on to remind us, "we are God's accomplishment, created in Christ Jesus to do good things. God planned for these good things to be the way that we live our lives" (Ephesians 2:10). The very Spirit of God has entered our lives so that we can take up once again the task that was ours in the story of Creation: to honor the image of God in our lives and to practice dominion over this world. We are called to imitate Christ and to enter deeply into the realities of this world and to bring healing and restoration wherever we walk. We are called to live humbly and to give of ourselves so that others—all others, including animals, plants, and the soil we walk on—might experience life.

Throughout this Advent season we have explored the hope of all of creation for restoration. We learned about how God clears a way for redemption in the midst of all that distracts us. We held in front of us the joy of the gifts of this creation if only we cherish and use them well. And we were reminded of the peace that comes when we love others the way that Christ loved us. This Christmas, all the earth is waiting for us to make room for the presence of God to dwell in all of creation.

Questions for Reflection and Discussion

1. John's Gospel tells us that the Word became flesh. What does it mean to you that God took on our physical reality?
2. What comfort does it bring to you that God has a plan?
3. How do you practice Sabbath in your life? Is it a time to get away from the world or a time to move closer to God in creation?
4. This study presented a different sort of Christmas narrative, that Jesus might have been born in a home instead of away from people in a barn. What does it mean that God might have been born in the midst of people and community?

5. What are some ways that the body of Christ in your community, your local church, can take up the call to practice dominion and care for this world?

Prayer

Holy God, the heavens and earth were formed so that you might dwell among us. You invited us in Sabbath rest to experience your presence, but we sought salvation in the busyness of our own making and doing. And so you entered our lives in the fullest of possible ways, in the birth of Jesus Christ. Help us, in this celebration of Christmas, to let you dwell in our lives and to take up our call to share your life with all of the world. Amen.

Focus for the Week

The season of Christmas is quickly followed by a new year and a time of resolution. What a wonderful opportunity to build new Sabbath practices into our lives. Prayerfully consider what kind of space you can carve out to spend intentional time in the presence of God. But also consider how you can express your deep care for the creation that surrounds you through this practice. Wayne Muller writes that, "Sabbath can only begin if we close the factory, turn out the lights, turn off the computer, and withdraw from the concerns of the marketplace."[12] And in many ways, the Jewish laws that formed around Sabbath were intended to allow Sabbath rest for other people, the animals, and the land itself. If during this time of Sabbath we refuse to use our cars or limit our energy consumption, if we eat food prepared with the soil in mind, if we refrain from consuming meat or only eat that which is ethically cared for, in all these ways, we can extend God's life to all of creation. This week, resolve to begin a new practice that will embody how you can live out the lessons of this study all year long.

WORSHIP RESOURCES FOR ADVENT AND CHRISTMAS

A Liturgy for Candle Lighting in the Advent Season

Creating, Redeeming, Sustaining God,
you formed us from the earth to love and obey you. In this season of waiting and expectation we look forward to the coming of your glory and the kingdom of God.

(week 1) **As we light this Advent candle, may we remember that hope comes from our trust in you, O God.**

(week 2) **As we light this Advent candle, may we remember that you have cleared the way for our salvation, O God.**

(week 3) **As we light this Advent candle, may we remember that when we pay attention, joyous gifts are all around us, O God.**

(week 4) **As we light this Advent candle, may we remember that peace will be found in the manger of Bethlehem, O God.**

(Christmas) **As we light the Christ candle, may we remember that you have come to dwell among us.**

A Prayer of Confession
for the Advent Season

Holy God, maker of this world and everything in it, all earth is waiting.

All earth is waiting for us to confess and repent of our selfish ways.

So in this season of longing and expectation, O God, we turn to you,
   seeking forgiveness, mercy, and strength for the challenges ahead.

(week 1) Where we have allowed fear and selfishness to drive us,
   fill us with hope so that your glory might be revealed.

(week 2) Where we have abused the resources of this planet,
   give us another way so that the gifts of creation might be
   shared with all.

(week 3) Where we have dishonored the abundance of the soil,
   remind us of the joy of sacramental use so that the land might
   be restored.

(week 4) Where we have become estranged from your created beings,
   teach us how to live in peace so that all might lie down in
   safety.

(Christmas) Where we have forgotten Your presence among us,
   call us once again to the gift of Sabbath so that we might
   experience the fullness of life.

All earth is waiting, breathless in expectation, to be set free.

Forgive us and transform our lives by the power of the Holy Spirit.
Amen.

A Call to Worship and Suggested Hymns
for Each Week of Advent

Week One: The Source of Hope

Call to Worship:

The nights around us grow longer,

But in you, O God, we hope.

The days are growing colder,

But in you, O God, we hope.

We are ever caught up in the cycles of life and death,

But in you, O God, we hope.

Gracious God, fill this time of worship with the promises of new life and help us carry your hope into the world.

Suggested Hymns:

Joy to the World

In the Bleak Midwinter

Creator of the Stars of Night

Angels from the Realms of Glory

O Holy Night

Hark! The Herald Angels Sing (consider including Wesley's stanzas 4 and 5, which can be found at https://en.wikipedia.org/wiki/Hark!_The_Herald_Angels_Sing).

Week Two: Clear the Way

Call to Worship:
In the wilderness, a voice calls out,
Clear the way!
In every valley and on every mountain,
Clear the way!
In places of clutter and chaos,
Clear the way!
Among the distractions and expectations,
Clear the way!
May God clear the way for us to fully worship this day.

Suggested Hymns:
My Soul Gives Glory to My God
People, Look East
Toda la Tierra (All Earth Is Waiting)
Wild and Lone the Prophet's Voice
Make Way

Week Three: Discovering Joy

Call to Worship:
Don't be afraid, comes the voice of the angel,
Rejoice and be glad!
Don't be afraid, say the prophets of old,
Rejoice and be glad!
Don't be afraid, but lift up your hearts,
Rejoice and be glad!

May we let go of fear, let go of scarcity, and embrace the abundance of God's blessings today.
Let us rejoice and be glad!

Suggested Hymns:
O Come, O Come, Emmanuel
Good Christian Friends, Rejoice
God Almighty, We Are Waiting
If I Could Visit Bethlehem
Joy to the World
Angels We Have Heard on High

Week Four: The Peace of the World

Call to Worship:
Along the paths of righteousness
A little child shall lead us.
Into the waters of justice,
A little child shall lead us.
Past the places of war into the fields of peace,
A little child shall lead us.
And his name is Emmanuel.
God with us.

Suggested Hymns:
The Friendly Beasts
The First Noel
Away in a Manger
Blessed Be the God of Israel
Welcome to Our World

Christmas: God Moves into the Neighborhood

Call to Worship:
On the seventh day of creation,
You came and lived among us.
As the Word became flesh,
You came and lived among us.
In the giving of the Holy Spirit,
You came and lived among us.
In the promise of the new creation,
You will come and live among us.
Holy God, in this moment of worship help us to open our lives to you,
So that we might become your body, your home, your life in this world.

Suggested Hymns:
God of Wonders
Hope Was Born This Night
One Holy Night in Bethlehem
Joseph Dearest, Joseph Mine
Thou Didst Leave Thy Throne
Glory in the Highest

NOTES

Chapter 1: The Source of Hope

1. Gayle Boss, "All Creation Waits," *On Being*, December 19, 2016. http://www.onbeing.org/blog/gayle-boss-all-creation-waits/9099.Accessed December 22, 2016.
2. Charles J. Chaput, " 'On Christian Hope' and Advent," Catholic News Agency, December 5, 2007. http://www.catholicnewsagency.com/resources/advent/bishops-previous-advent-teachings/on-christian-hope-and-advent/. Accessed December 2, 2016.
3. Joseph Sittler, "Nature and Grace in Romans 8," in *Evocations of Grace: The Writings of Joseph Sittler on Ecology, Theology, and Ethics*, edited by Steven Bouma-Prediger and Peter W. Bakken (Grand Rapids: Eerdmans, 2000), 213-214.
4. Brenden Busse, S.J. "Grace Enough" *America*. http://www.americamagazine.org/issue/grace-enough. Accessed May 17, 2017.
5. Ibid.
6. *The New Interpreter's Bible*, Volume X, (Nashville: Abingdon Press, 2015) 524.
7. *The New Interpreter's Bible*, Volume I (Nashville: Abingdon Press, 2015), 349.
8. Joseph Sittler, 211.
9. "Saint Francis and the Birds," https://www.franciscanmedia.org/saint-francis-and-the-birds/. Accessed May 18, 2017.
10. Ibid.

Chapter 2: Clear the Way

1. *The New Interpreter's Bible*, Volume IXIX (Nashville: Abingdon Press, 1996), 56.
2. *The New Interpreter's Bible*, Volume VI (Nashville: Abingdon Press, 2001), 338.
3. *The New Interpreter's Bible*, Volume VIIVII (Nashville: Abingdon Press, 2015), 156.
4. Nash Dunn, "Research Seeks Answers to Black Lung Resurgence in Central Appalachia." https://news.ncsu.edu/2015/12/black-lung-2015/. Accessed May 19, 2017.
5. Howard Berkes, "Advanced Black Lung Cases Surge in Appalachia," *All Things Considered*, December 15, 2016. http://www.npr .org/2016/12/15/505577680/advanced-black-lung-cases-surge-in/ -appalachia. Accessed May 19, 2017.
6. *The New Interpreter's Bible*, Volume VI, 335.
7. Joseph Sittler, *The Eloquence of Grace: Joseph Sittler and the Preaching Life*, edited by James M. Childs Jr. and Richard Lischer (Eugene, OR: Cascade Books, an Imprint of Wipf and Stock Publishers, 2012), 24.
8. Ibid., 24-25.
9. Ibid., 25.
10. Henri Nouwen, *Thomas Merton: Contemplative Critic* (Liguori, MO: Liguori Publications, 1991), 24.

Chapter 3: Discovering Joy

1. *The New Interpreter's Bible*, Volume VII, 305.
2. Ibid., 324.
3. Dan Barber, *The Third Plate: Field Notes on the Future of Food* (New York: Penguin Books, 2014), 48.
4. Ibid., 70.
5. Ibid., 72.
6. Ibid., 41.
7. *The New Interpreter's Bible*, Volume VII, 325.
8. Joseph Sittler, "The Care of the Earth," in *Evocations of Grace*, 58.

Chapter 4: The Peace of the World

1. John Wesley, "The General Deliverance," I.3. http://wesley.nnu.edu /john-wesley/the-sermons-of-john-wesley-1872-edition/sermon -60-the-general-deliverance/.
2. *The New Interpreter's Bible*, Volume I, 346.

3. Ibid., 357.
4. John Wesley, II.2.
5. Ibid., II.3.
6. Ibid.
7. "A Friend in the Midst of Nature's Harder Edge," http://taprootgarden .blogspot.com/2017/01/a-friend-in-midst-of-natures-harder-edge.html. Accessed May 19, 2017.
8. Terence E. Fretheim, "Commentary on Genesis 9:8-17" for *Working Preacher.* http://www.workingpreacher.org/preaching .aspx?commentary_id=253. Accessed May 24, 2017.
9. *The New Interpreter's Bible,* Volume I, 398.
10. John Wesley, II.6
11. Elizabeth Johnson, "For God so loved the cosmos," *U.S. Catholic,* April 2010. http://www.uscatholic.org/culture/environment/2010/07/ god-so-loved-world-jesus-and-environment. Accessed May 19, 2017.
12. *The Sword and the Trowel: A Record of Combat with Sin and of Labour for the Lord,* ed. C. H. Spurgeon, (London: Passmore & Alabaster, 1873), 242.
13. *The New Interpreter's Bible,* Volume VI, 141.
14. John Wesley, III.3.

Chapter 5: God Moves into the Neighborhood

1. Wayne Muller, *Sabbath: Finding Rest, Renewal, and Delight in our Busy Lives* (New York: Bantam, 2000), 78-79.
2. Jürgen Moltmann, *God in Creation* (Minneapolis: Augsburg Fortress, 1993), 280.
3. Ibid., 279
4. Wayne Muller, 9.
5. Ibid., 32.
6. Joseph Sittler, "A Theology for Earth," in *Evocations of Grace,* 29.
7. Parker J. Palmer, *Let Your Life Speak: Listening for the Voice of Vocation* (San Francisco: Jossey-Bass, 2000), 84-85.
8. Keith Innes, http://www.greenchristian.org.uk/lectionary1. Accessed May 19, 2017.
9. Jürgen Moltmann, 183-184.
10. *The New Interpreter's Bible,* Volume XI (Nashville: Abingdon Press, 2000), 360.
11. Jürgen Moltmann, 172.
12. Wayne Muller, 27.

CPSIA information can be obtained
at www.ICGtesting.com
Printed in the USA
LVOW10s2245310517
536493LV00005B/15/P